MAKING SCHOOLS THAT ARE GOOD FOR KIDS

CREATING A DEMOCRATIC SOCIETY

TOM DURRIE

Free School Press

Also by Tom Durrie

School and the End of Intelligence:
The Erosion of Civilized Society

The beauty of this book is found in its alternating current of fury and compassion, realism and hope, humour and common sense. It is an exceptional ride.—Dr Charles Barber (MA, DMA Stanford) Author of *Corresponding With Carlos: A Biography of Carlos Kleiber* (Rowman and Littlefield)

This is a fascinating read even for those well-versed in the legacy of great authors in the field of educational freedom. The book is jam-packed with curious tidbits from all imaginable sources to boost core theses of the author. In his exposure of human ignorance, the author's caustic language is likely to make you laugh more than once.
--Piotr Wozniak, PhD, *SuperMemo Research*, Poland

Read this book. Filled with facts and astute humorous observations, this book exposes the many ironic results of school.— Marty Layne, homeschool mom of four, author of *Learning At Home: A Mother's Guide To Homeschooling, Newly Revised Edition*

Durrie brings together an impressive array of contexts and disciplines including game theory, merchandising, psychology, philosophy, and music to illustrate his major point that school systems as currently structured are the worst possible places to get an education.—Jak King, *historian, author, blogger*, Vancouver, BC

This book is absolutely excellent!! Would recommend anyone with soon-to-be school age children to read it. Your children will thank you forever. A most amazing book and so easy to read.— Gail Paquette, Abbotsford, BC

Available from *Free School Press*
freeschoolpress@proton.me

Thank God, I never was sent to School
To be Flogg'd into following the Stile of a Fool.
--William Blake

A NOTE TO THE READER

I suppose I shouldn't start with explanations (excuses?), but this book has gone through so many changes and permutations that I will never be completely satisfied with it. It started out with the master's thesis of 2001 that I wrote for Prescott College, but I soon saw that it was outdated and far from complete, at least to my present state of mind. There are still bits and pieces of it here and there, especially the quotes from Lady Allen and Carolyn Pratt. Reading their statements about children and education, I'm sure you'll see what remarkable women they must have been. And if you've read my other book, you'll know that I'm a fan of Frank Smith, so you're going to encounter him again and again in this book.

The first subtitle of this book was *The End of School Slavery*, but I wanted to change the focus to democracy, how schools are anti-democratic and how the school I'm proposing would be not just pro-democratic, but democratic in practice. That involved some rewriting and adding here and there. I hope this aspect of the book will come through loud and clear. Democracy and rule of law are at risk in many nations as people turn to right-wing demagogues, hoping for salvation. We teach children in school that they have no rights and then expect them to participate in a democratic society.

I also worry about being repetitious. Are there too many tropes about freedom, learn-from-the-company-you-keep, and how bad school is? These are matters I keep hitting on, but how else to express my solid belief in the goodness of human nature, the innate power of children's learning, and the urgent need for change?

Tom

ISBN   978-1-7389351-1-6

Free School Press
PO Box 299
Boston Bar, BC
Canada
V0K 1C0
freeschoolpress@proton.me

TABLE OF CONTENTS

MAKING SCHOOLS
THAT ARE GOOD FOR KIDS
Creating a Democratic Society

Introduction

Can there be any doubt that society is in trouble? Only slightly more than half of eligible voters actually cast a ballot; many people who don't vote say that they are simply not interested in politics or that their vote won't matter; many people believe that politicians are not trustworthy; literacy is waning, newspapers are virtually non-existent as readership has declined; authoritarian right-wing populist movements are on the rise; audiences for serious art and musical events are vanishing; popular songs are devoted to juvenile sentiments with little musical value; sports heroes are lauded as the main source of national pride; social media are inundated with trivia and false information, conspiracy theories abound; incidents of racial prejudice and hatred are on the rise; gun violence is epidemic in the United States where 327 people are shot every day, including 23 children; drug use is such that 21 people die of overdose every day in Canada; in schools, bullying is on the increase; suicide is the second leading cause of death among children and young adults; in schools, violence particularly against teachers, is an increasing problem; attention spans are drastically decreasing as people spend more time gazing at screens; young children are mesmerized by idiotic and chaotic computer-created cartoons. It seems that no one wants to work anymore. Are we losing a sense of the dignity of work, self-support, and collaboration in the com-

monwealth of the community? Is it true that as Robert Put-
man suggests, we are *Bowling Alone*?[1]

In most western countries, people spend twelve or more
years of their young lives in an authoritarian dictatorial institution called school. They emerge unprepared to participate
in a democratic society often with little knowledge of the
workings of government and a distrust of all authority. I am
suggesting that school is responsible for the deterioration of
political discourse and participation in democratic society.
This is why my book *School and the End of* Intelligence is subti-
tled *The Erosion of Civilized* Society. How else could it be since
schools fail so miserably at their proclaimed purposes? All
efforts to increase literacy, reduce prejudice, inculcate decency
and good manners, or stop bullying are having the opposite
effect. And yet, children are spending more and more time
under the influence of school. Daycare and preschool are taking up the early part of childhood to the extent that at least
fifteen years of a young person's life are spent under the influence of school. It's time to consider an alternative.

This book is about a school that has no classes, no
grades, no tests, no marks, and no teachers.[2] Decisions regarding conduct, behaviour, and community relations will be
made by democratic assembly in which each person, regardless of age or position, has one vote. Is this a school that is
good for kids? Would it be good for society? Obviously I
think so or I wouldn't be writing this book. And, also obvi-

---

[1] Robert D. Putnam, *Bowling Alone, The Collapse and Revival of
American Community*, (New York: Simon & Schuster Paperbacks,
2000).
[2] Teachers, in the sense of individuals who are certified in how-to-teach
without having any particular area of expertise of their own.

ously, I believe that schools as they now exist are *not* good for kids—or anyone else.

In this book I will address what might replace the schools that have dominated the lives of the young for the past 150 years or so, and are now, with the growth of institutional day-care and preschool, insinuating their ideals of child management into our daily lives, especially the lives of our children.

The school system cannot be "reformed." Only a radical transformation can make a difference.

School as we know it is based on an outdated established social order; it is not there for the benefit of children, except if we see them only as imperfect beings in need of correction, direction, discipline, and constant surveillance. We are the only species that considers our young incapable of following instinctual drives toward growth, learning, and participation in society. Who else seeks out the direction of books, classes, and advice-givers for the nurture and instruction of the young? Following the dictates of society, at age six or younger, children will be handed over to nearly full-time management by various certified experts. School now takes charge of training children to take part in an imaginary authoritarian society based on the ethics and principles of the nineteenth century factory. Children in school have no rights, only certain privileges that may be granted.

In every society, the education, training, and rearing of the young are functions of parents, elders, and other trusted grown-ups. Instead, we have chosen to institutionalize our children for this purpose. But in or out of school, the young are learning by observing and identifying with others. Often, or even always, they are learning from what they observe, not from what they are taught. In societies that we think of as primitive there is no fabricated structure for the training of the young. They learn what they need to learn by working and playing alongside their elders. In earlier times, before school,

15

our youngsters learned about being grown-up from working beside their parents, other adults in their family, and artisans and workers in their community. In the evening the family gathered around to read and to listen to reading, most likely from the newspaper or the King James Bible. Learning was a natural and organic part of growing up. Children were active participants in family and working life.

This started to change when school, with compulsory attendance, was devised, in eighteenth century Prussia, to control the peasantry, produce compliant workers, and obedient young men for the military. For this purpose, an arbitrary curriculum was determined and imposed upon the young who now had no choice about what to do or what to learn. Nobody wanted the peasants to think they had any say in how their lives were managed. Isn't this still the structure of the schools of today? Peasants = Children.

In the nineteenth and early twentieth centuries school served the purpose of providing disciplined and trained workers for the factories and offices of cities, at the same time denigrating intellectual, artistic, and emotional life along with originality and creativity that might lead to criticism of the established order. School infantilizes the young until they are deemed certifiable and disciplined enough to be released into the adult world. Schools and the people who run them must believe without question that this is just the way things are. What with the world crumbling around us with seemingly uncontrollable phenomena like runaway technology, violence, hate, drug use, ignorance, inequality, climate change, and just plain stupidity, the call for trained and obedient workers seems out of place. In any endeavour at all, what's needed are people of intelligence, imagination, creativity, and curiosity. The very attributes that have been downplayed if not squelched entirely by the kind of schooling we have been subjecting our kids to.

It's time for something completely different.

A Bit of History

The introduction of compulsory public schooling meant that learning now became the province of educational experts. Parents were told that they were not able to teach their children anything as complicated as reading or arithmetic. These subjects now became arcane mysteries accessible only through certified professionals. Children were removed from their homes for the greater part of the day and housed in special institutions which were to train them in the knowledge and skills they would need to take part in adult society.

At first many parents were reluctant to send their kids to a school that was not part of their community. The one-room schoolhouse that was an integral part of family and social life had served their educational needs for many years. Attendance was flexible, advancement was based on individual progress, and the one teacher, known to everyone, was resident in the community. But now, parental reluctance had to be overcome by laws, sometimes enforced at gunpoint, making school attendance compulsory. The one-room school was replaced by the large city school with its graded classrooms, certified teachers, and regimental discipline. Children in rural communities then had to be delivered to the distant school by bus, depriving them of an additional hour or more at either end of their day and effectively removing them from the lives of their parents and other grownups.

The first North American school system, fully controlled by the government, was based on the principles of Prussian schools as observed by Horace Mann in 1843. He was successful in lobbying to have this system adopted by Massachusetts schools in 1882. Canada followed suit and all schools soon adopted Prussian methods.[3]

But wait a minute, not everyone thought that this was all such a good idea. Argument soon arose over strict discipline and top-down instruction versus emphasis on the child's needs and interests. Notions of child-centred education were introduced by John Dewey as early as the 1890s. But this was not exactly new because similar approaches to education had been proposed by Jean-Jacques Rousseau (1712-1778), Johann Pestalozzi (1746-1827), and others. None of these proposals, including those of John Dewey, have had any lasting effect on the way schools define education, in spite of the various changes and reforms that have been tried over the years.

Everything seemed to be going along more or less smoothly, with a bit of this and a bit of that, until 1912 when schools came under harsh attack by magazines and newspapers proclaiming the failure of schools to produce disciplined workers. Teachers had been placing far too much emphasis on the interests and wishes of the child, forgetting that their job was supposed to be to inculcate the predetermined goals of school learning. Under the then popular scientific efficiency ideas of Frederick Taylor, schools turned toward set curricula, top-down instruction, and standardized testing. Pupils were expected to march lock-step through the process of being educated.

Well, as it turned out, that didn't work so well either, so theories about child-centred education began to re-emerge in the 1940s. The watchwords, again based on the writings of John Dewey, were now *teach the whole child, experiential learning,* and *child-centred education.*

---

[3] For a detailed discussion of such methods, see my other book, *School and the End of Intelligence.*

By now, you've probably got the idea that our school systems have swung back and forth between the rigid and the flexible. And, sure enough, the next revolution came with the ominous beeping of Sputnik, the first space satellite, launched by (shudder) the Soviet Union. Schools, under the influence of so-called progressive education, had failed to provide the country with enough well-trained mathematicians and scientists to compete in the space race. We'd better tighten up and put those kids in their place! This led to such disastrous government programs (in the U.S.) as *No Child Left Behind*, *Unlocking Our Future*, and *A Nation at Risk*.

With the publication, in 1960, of A. S. Neill's *Summerhill*, a new wave of criticism of the school system was underway. Writers like Ivan Illich, Paul Goodman, John Holt, A. S. Neill, James Hearndon, and Edgar Friedenberg criticized the system for being repressive and irrelevant. "Turn on, tune in, and drop out," was the motto of 1960s youth culture that regarded the grown-up world as narrow minded, "uptight," and responsible for the ills of the world, especially the war in Vietnam. One result, however short-lived, was the creation of so-called "free schools," based to one degree or another on A. S. Neill's Summerhill School in Leiston, England. As free schools sprang up here and there, many people failed to see anything good about them. The kids were a ragtag bunch, clothed any old which way, and running around discussing political and social issues, often with alarming confidence and courage. Something had to be done. So public schools co-opted some diluted principles of Summerhill, many kids reentered "the system," and the independent free school movement died out. It really comes down to depriving kids of the rights to which they are entitled in a democratic society.

One positive result of this flurry of free thinking about schooling was the abolition of the strap in most provinces. The supreme court of Canada finally ruled that corporal pun-

19

ishment was an unreasonable application of force in the maintenance of classroom discipline—but not until 2004. However, at the same time the court upheld the "right" of parents to brutalize their children by spanking—as long as it didn't leave any bruises! Disciplining of children through corporal punishment is still allowed in many U.S. states and other parts of the world.

Once again, as the twentieth century drew to a close, a wave of conservatism swept through society and through the schools. Preparation for a profitable profession and for status in society was now seen as the goal of education. The neoliberal economic policies of Ronald Reagan and Margaret Thatcher imbued society with a belief in market-based competition. The rebellious optimism of the 1960s was replaced by emphasis on career goals and STEM (Science, Technology, Engineering, Mathematics). Many parents again believed that the public schools were too lax, that standards were too low. They lobbied for stricter schools with emphasis on drill and discipline, believing that this kind of school was the only way to prepare their children for the tough competition of university entrance and the world of technology and business. While this has been going on, writers like Alfie Kohn, John Taylor Gatto, Peter Grey, Ken Robinson, and Frank Smith have addressed issues of intelligence and learning that have been critical of the way public schools attempt to educate. And now, the populism of the 2020s promotes a strange kind of antidemocratic individualism and disdain of established order. What that means for school is yet to be seen, but certain liberal trends have prompted many parents to yank their kids out of school. What will happen is anyone's guess.

With all this in mind, I have surveyed and reported on significant theories of learning and intelligence, and I have looked at two social phenomena which I believe are significant factors in how we should plan the education of our young. These are technology and the changing relation of youth to adults in our culture. I have then presented my own argument against the existence of the kind of schooling we have had since the introduction of compulsory public schooling in the mid nineteenth century. This leads to the final chapter which is an attempt to describe a radically different kind of school that would capitalize on children's innate drive to learn from their surroundings and to become actively engaged in the society in which they find themselves.

BRAIN, MIND, INTELLIGENCE, AND LEARNING

For all children life should be ... a continuous celebration free from the pressures which can do irreparable damage to their self-esteem.—Lady Allen[4]

The process of re-thinking school would sensibly begin with an understanding of how the process of learning works and of how intelligence is developed.

While there is a growing body of knowledge about how the physical brain grows and functions, just how experiences are processed and amalgamated into what we call "mind" and "intelligence" seem to elude scientific examination. We can say that learning is a process involving the entire organism, including all the behaviours which a keen observer may perceive as well as the emotions and attitudes that are not always open to observation.

Three Stories

When three-year-old James comes with his father to visit from time to time, the first thing he wants to know is if the "pimputer" is on. Since it usually is, I close down any documents I may have been working on, and he takes his place at the keyboard. He is fascinated by the idea that touching the keys makes things happen on the screen in front of him. He crows with delight as he holds down one key and the letters race across the screen. Having received minimal instruction,

---

[4] Marjory Allen & Mary Nicholson, *Memoirs of an Uneducated Lady: Lady Allen of Hurtwood,* (London: Thames and Hudson Ltd, 1975), 43.

he is very careful to depress only one key at a time. But his curiosity is such that he wants to try them all, one by one. I once showed him how to find the print icon with the mouse arrow and how to click in order to set the printer into action. With a little practice, he was able to print his pages of run-on letters, though this seemed to hold less excitement for him than controlling the action on the screen.

My son Miles, before he was two years old, figured out how to arrange a set of nesting boxes he had into a convenient stairway that would allow him access to just about any out-of-reach spot in the house. His curiosity and desire to be involved were so intense that within seconds he could assemble and mount his stairs and be right in the midst of whatever grown-up activity might be going on.

When I was four, my playmate Bobby and I would spend a good deal of time "painting" a derelict galvanized water tank that lay in his backyard. For some reason, there were a couple of abandoned paint brushes nearby and a can filled with rain water. Our painting consisted of spreading the water over the surface of the tank. The fact that it was water, not paint, and that it would soon evaporate, was never an issue in the gravity and industry with which we worked.

These three stories illustrate important aspects of children's learning, all of which involve real work, intense emotional involvement, and a sense of accomplishment in the act itself. James's work with the computer is based on his apparent desire to make it "go." He is not particularly interested in either watching me type on the computer or in being instructed in its other features. He wants to do it himself. For the moment, he does what he can do best, and he finds great joy in his association with the machine. What he is doing is to him real work. After all, when he sees me working at the computer, what am I doing other than making letters run across the screen? The fact that I am spelling out words and sentences is to him irrelevant. The main event is the very action of operating a machine and making things happen. And that's what he wants to do, too. John Dewey, as if he knew James personally, writes about little children's learning,

> Their minds seek wholes, varied through episode, enlivened with action and defined in salient features—there must be go, movement, the sense of use and operation—inspection of things separated from the idea by which they are carried. Analysis of isolated detail of form and structure neither appeals nor satisfies.[5]

Arranging blocks or sticks or dolls in order of size is known by researchers as "seriation," and according to Margaret Boden, Jean Piaget, who spent a lifetime studying children's learning behaviour and intellectual development believed that a child of three or four "is quite unable to build a 'staircase' of blocks with a set of seven blocks provided for her."[6] Not being acquainted with Piaget, my son Miles was able to arrange his boxes into an effective staircase out of his intense, almost fierce, desire to participate in and not be left out of household activities in spite of his diminutive stature. His accomplishment was directed toward a goal of urgent importance to him, and it emerged in a context of real work, not an artificially constructed experiment.

And finally, as Bobby and I "painted" the water tank, we were seriously engaged in the process and work of using the tools of painting as we had observed big people doing. The act of painting was the important thing. Whether or not we actually covered the tank with a lasting coat of paint was as

---

[5] John Dewey, *The School and Society; The Child and the Curriculum, Reprint, Centennial edition,* (Chicago: University of Chicago Press: 1990), 140.
[6] Margaret Boden, *Piaget,* (London: Fontana Press, 1994), 56.

irrelevant as word-processing is to James or seriation to Miles. We were experimenting with how work was done in the grown-up world.

The Mechanics of Learning

Learning, whether it's water painting or nuclear physics depends upon the awesome power and capacity of the human brain. This relatively small organ, weighing under 1.4 kilograms, has been called the most complex structure in the universe. It enables humans to perform such feats as speaking sixteen or more different languages, memorizing the New Testament, or playing from memory all forty-eight preludes and fugues of Bach's *Well-Tempered Clavier*. And these are really only stunts of memory. Even a relatively simple computer is able to remember and process more information than any brain. However, the circuitry that enables the staggering complexity of the *creation* of the *Well-Tempered Clavier*, the translation (into superb Shakespearean English) of the New Testament, and the *invention* of computers and 747s is truly awe-inspiring. As sophisticated as artificial intelligence has become, a computer is not yet capable of creating its own symbols and its own culture and a philosophy by which to contemplate its self. No amount of analysis of the circuitry of the brain has yet explained the *emotional* impact of the music of Beethoven, the sonnets of Shakespeare, or the raptures of falling in love.

Facial recognition software now makes it possible for a computer to identify an individual face, but it can tell us nothing about the emotional or psychological impact that face may have on another human being. It is well known that we respond, often subconsciously, to facial cues and minute variations in expression. Many animals are also good at this, as anyone with a dog or cat will tell you. We quickly identify friend or foe—or fall in love at first sight. Will a computer ever know this experience? I hope not.

Though sophisticated technologies such as the PET (positron emission tomography) scans are revealing many details about the functioning of the brain, they can tell us nothing about consciousness, mind, or emotion. Other devices that measure heart rate and sweat production can tell us that an emotional state may be heightened, but little or nothing about what this *means* to the individual being measured.

By the time of birth, the physical substance of the brain and nervous system, with 100 billion neurons(!), is complete, and the "wiring phase" begins. Wiring involves establishing countless electrical circuits of varying strength, with each neuron typically interacting with some ten thousand others. This process begins even before birth and continues throughout life, though most of the shaping of the brain takes place during the first five years. This is the process we call "learning," and most of it takes place **subconsciously and effortlessly**. We don't have to *teach* our kids to talk and to walk.

The basic structure of a neuron is about the same as that of any other cell in the body except for certain features. Each neuron is built of three parts: the cell body, the axon, and the dendrites. It is by means of the axon and dendrites that the neuron is able to communicate with other neurons by means of electrical impulses. While some neurons are adapted and dedicated to specific functions, such as sight or touch, millions of others are available for use as required by the developing organism.

The axon, or nerve fibre, is a hair-like structure from one millimetre to one metre in length, through which a small electrical signal of approximately 70 millivolts is fired from the cell's nucleus when stimulated by an external signal like sight, touch, sound, or by internal messages about hunger, loneli-

27

ness, satiety, temperature, etc. This signal then passes to other neurons via the dendrites, which cluster like a hairy web around each cell's nucleus. The axon is not in actual physical contact with the dendrites, the space between being known as a synapse. Impulses cross the synapse by means of chemical substances known as neurotransmitters.

As stimuli impinge upon the organism, neurons send impulses firing across synapses. The more powerful the stimulus, the more urgent the impulse, the stronger and more lasting becomes the synaptic connection. In other words, as experiences are repeated or strengthened by emotion, the neurotransmitters that pass the impulse across the synapse become more efficient and more reliable, and the connection becomes more firmly established. Over fifty different neurotransmitters have been identified, and there is reason to believe that they are closely associated, if not directly identified, with emotion. If the developing brain is infused with love, tenderness, acceptance, and fulfillment, its synapses will be charged with positive experiences, growth, and cognitive development. If, on the other hand, emotions are overwhelmed with anxiety and frustration, coping mechanisms will overpower growth and development. In the first case you will see an individual who is comfortable with other people and will be concerned about the well-being of others. And in the second case, a person of suspicion, distrust, and hostility.

The role of emotion in learning is one of those elusive ideas, like that of mind or intellect that seems evident yet does not lend itself to research or experimentation. Nevertheless, the emotional engagement in the stories of our young workers suggests that powerful forces are at work.

Two-year-old Miles was not only building stairways but also strong synaptic connections contributing to his understanding of geometry, size, number, height, and space, as well as his personal feelings of accomplishment and capability, positive emotions that would henceforth be associated with the concepts he was learning. He experienced his curiosity, and then industriously constructed a way to satisfy it. James is developing a relationship with the computer and, at the same time, a sense of elation over his ability to control this exciting machine. The brains of Bobby and me were, as we co-operatively applied ourselves to our work, being wired in the areas of eye-hand coordination and the manipulation of tools. Imagine how these positive growth experiences would have been hampered and perverted by the imposition of instruction or discipline.

Piaget vs. Vygotsky

Two notable observers of infant and child growth were the contemporaries Jean Piaget (1896-1980) and Lev Vygotsky (1896-1934). Both developed theories of cognitive development in children that the education experts have seized to elaborate methods of instruction. Piaget's schema of growth is still the most influential in how schools organize classes and plan lessons. Fair enough, I suppose, because Piaget came first, although he and Vygotsky were working and even publishing at the same time. Vygotsky's work has been slower to come to the front because it was slow to be translated from the Russian, and Vygotsky died before his writings were polished and complete.

As opposed to the earlier notion propounded by thinkers like John Locke (1632-1704) that the young mind was simply a blank slate upon which experience would leave its mark, Piaget developed the idea that the child is actively involved in his or her own development. Thus, at even the earliest stage of growth, reflex responses, such as sucking and grasping, initiate and direct the infant's exploration of the environment.

The tiny hand will soon grasp mother's finger, and the mouth will move toward the nipple and form the shape for sucking. These and other actions then become refined and perfected as the infant grows and "works on" them, a process which has been described as a "basic need for exercising one's capacities;"[7] In short, Piaget introduced the idea that infants were not passive receptacles of experience but active seekers of stimulation with which to develop their physical and mental abilities.

But the real clincher in his theory was the definition of four stages of growth, with ages at which each stage could be expected to appear. Thus:

COGNITIVE DEVELOPMENT

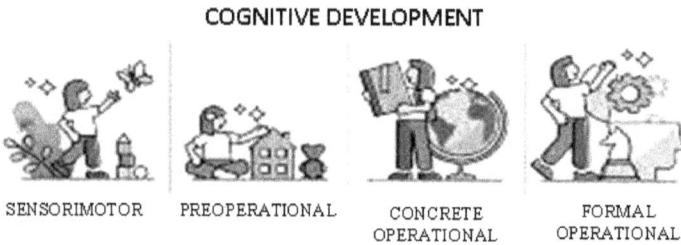

| SENSORIMOTOR | PREOPERATIONAL | CONCRETE OPERATIONAL | FORMAL OPERATIONAL |

Age 0-2 the *Sensorimotor Stage*. The child experiences the world mostly through sensory impressions and motor activities.

Age 2-7 the *Pre-operational Stage*. The child begins to master language but can't yet perform mental operations.

Age 7-12 the *Concrete Operational Stage*. Here the youngster can be expected to understand how things work, but cannot yet think abstractly.

Age 12-adulthood the *Formal Operational Stage*. Here's where abstract thinking, like coming up with ideas, weighing possibilities, and passing judgment, comes into play.

---

[7] Boden, *Piaget*, 22.

While this is about as condensed and simple an explanation of Piaget as you'll find, I hope it will give you the basic idea of rating cognitive development by stages. And you can quickly see how school segregates children by age accordingly. This is the method by which curriculum planners decide what kind of learning is suited to each grade or age group, but the idea of the child as an active participant in his own development seems to have been dropped along the way.

In almost direct contradiction to Piaget, Lev Vygotsky wrote:

> Our concept of development implies a rejection of the frequently held view that cognitive development results from the gradual accumulation of separate changes. We believe that child development is a complex dialectical process characterized by periodicity, unevenness in the development of different functions, metamorphosis or qualitative transformation of one form into another, intertwining of external and internal factors, and adaptive processes which overcome impediments that the child encounters.[8]

Though Vygotsky's work has been little known, his concepts of growth and development focus on person to person interactions rather than exploration of environment. Whereas Piaget emphasized learning by hands-on experience with social interaction being a diversion, Vygotsky turns our attention to connections with other people. To me, this means that the emotional content of relationships, e.g. mother and child, is what determines the emerging structure of the brain. Of course, as Vygotsky points out, development has its many ins and outs, but as I have said before, children will inevitably react and adapt to the atmosphere created by the people

---

[8] L. S. Vygotsky, *Mind in Society, The Development of Higher Psychological Processes,* ed. Michael Cole, Vera John-Steiner, Sylvia Scribner, Ellen Souberman. (Cambridge, MA: Harvard University Press, 1978), 73.

around them. I should mention that under adverse circumstances that adaptation may become one of rebellion or self-suppression.

Vygotsky emphasized the importance of language. After all, the syntax and grammar of our language determine how we interpret reality and experience. How often do we fall into the trap of not recognizing differences in culture as realized in language. What does it mean to be an Italian, growing up speaking and thinking only Italian, as opposed to being, say, Chinese? (Does the adjective come before or after the noun it describes? Does the verb come at the end or in the middle of a sentence? Are there formal and informal forms of address?) Language determines not only how we say things but also how we think about things. The grammar and syntax of language determine cultural differences that often result in misunderstandings if not conflict.

An aspect of Vygotsky's theory that has been applied by schools, wherever possible, is the Zone of Proximal Development. It suggests that the space between what a learner can do without assistance can be filled with what a learner can do in collaboration with more advanced or more knowledgeable others. Learning, according to the Vygotsky model, means there is a drive to learn more and more all the time since the boundaries between the "zones" are flexible and always changing. The richer the middle zone of the circle the more learning will take place and the more the outer zone (inability) will change to ability. To quote from Frank Smith, "It is not difficult to see how learning flourishes when there is interest, confidence, and understanding and how it withers under boredom, trepidation, and confusion."[9] Teachers take note.

---

[9] Frank Smith, *The Book of Learning and Forgetting*. (New York: Teachers College Press. 1998), 85.

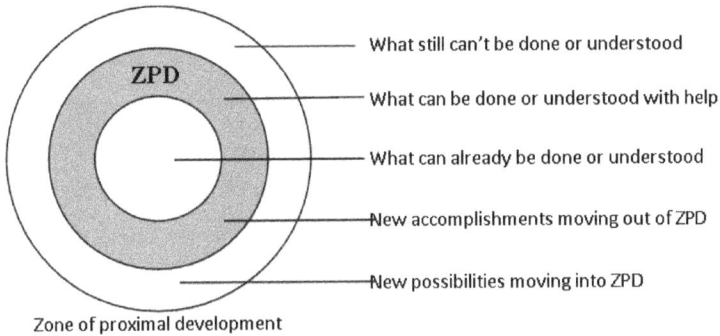

ZPD

What still can't be done or understood

What can be done or understood with help

What can already be done or understood

New accomplishments moving out of ZPD

New possibilities moving into ZPD

Zone of proximal development

Above all the richness of the middle and outer zones must come from the other people with whom the child associates. Those "other people" need not be present in person. They can be authors, composers, characters in movies or on television. Need I mention the destructive and confusing effects of the so-called educational toys and videos. What are children learning from idiotic puppets, garish plastic toys, and simplistic repetitive computer-generated music? Remember when children were addressed like intelligent human beings by such people as Fred Rogers and Bob Homme (The Friendly Giant)? Real people talking to children without patronizing or condescending.

My position, as always, is that children (and everyone else) learn best when given a free rein to explore and engage their environment. The more directing and teaching there is, the more learning will be hindered. This is not to say that we don't learn from others, even teachers, but instruction and assistance are only useful when asked for. Learning takes place through observation, engagement, and participation.

Inspired by Piaget, the American psychologist and pediatrician Arnold Gesell developed theoretical constructs of cognitive development that have been seized upon to set standards of what is normal for children of any given age. Gesell, along with Frances Ilg, created a comprehensive theory of infant and child growth that set down certain characteristics to be expected at given ages. Not only did this send parents scurrying to the checklists to see if their child was "normal," but also provided schools with a "scientific" justification for setting "age appropriate" curricular goals. Any child who strayed too far from those goals was judged as abnormal, or, as they would prefer to say, "learning disabled." Such children may also be judged to have psychological problems that call for some kind of intervention. This created an entirely new field of child psychologists, specialized remedial teachers, and pharmaceuticals.

Considering the staggering accomplishments, largely untutored, made during the first five years of life, it is not unreasonable to conclude that there is an irresistible drive or need to assimilate and perfect the skill and knowledge required to become a functioning individual in whatever environment one finds oneself. By the age of five, most children have mastered the grammar and syntax of at least one language, and sometimes more than one, have learned to walk upright and navigate uneven terrain, can distinguish friends from foes, are able to form original ideas and concepts, understand notions of quantity and size, and so on. Given half a chance, many children this age will also teach themselves to read. In other words, by this tender age, the child will have acquired all the major and most difficult skills needed to live an effective life. I might add that some children achieve this level, or close to it, against all odds: poverty, absent parents, abuse of one kind or another, malnutrition, mistreatment, and physical handicap. The drive to learn is *that* powerful.

All this being said however, we can slice and dice children's behaviours all we want but we will end up playing a mug's game of defining a fictitious child and applying certain developmental standards whether they exist or not. Thus, we start seeing life as a Bell Curve with "normal" in the middle and aberrant behaviours on either side. This provides an excuse for designing curricula, teaching methods, and segregation by chronological age. A pointless and counterproductive attempt to steer children's development the way the school wants.

I think Rousseau had it right when, in 1763, he wrote:

> A means surer than all these, and the one always forgotten, is the desire to learn. Give your child this desire, then let your desks and your dice go. Any method will be good for him.[10]

Perhaps "Give your child this desire" is misleading because the desire to learn is already there. It comes with the package. Let's say *allow* the desire to learn. And I would hasten to add that a desire to learn cannot be forced or cleverly motivated. At least we are deluding ourselves if we think so. A. S. Neill, reflective of Rousseau, had this to say on the subject of *how-to-teach* children to perform:

> Whether a school has or has not a special method for teaching long division is of no significance, for long division is of no importance except to those who want to learn it. And the child who wants to learn long division will learn it no matter how it is taught.[11]

What I derive from Rousseau, Vygotsky, Neill and others is that cognitive development, growth, and learning cannot be slotted into stages or grades. Learning is the work of the developing brain of the child, and every child will be different in every way. Real learning is messy, random, and unstoppable. As A. S. Neill is famously quoted as saying, "Take care of the heart and the gizzard, and the brain will look after itself." Or

---

[10] Jean Jacques Rousseau, *Emile or On Education, trans Allan Bloom,* (New York: Basic Books Inc, 1979), 117.
[11] Alexander S. Neill, *Summerhill, A Radical Approach to Childrearing,* (New York: Hart Publishing Company: 1960), 4-5.

as he wrote, perhaps more politely: "If the emotions are free, the intellect will look after itself."[12]

My homeschooler friend Marty Layne said, "I don't know how children learn, they just do."

Thinking and Feeling

The child psychiatrist Stanley Greenspan (1941-2010) pointed out that both Piaget and Freud regarded thought and emotion as separate functions, and that rational thought (ego) could somehow control rampant emotion (libido). He goes on to say, "Because of this dichotomy, our culture has an immense, longstanding intellectual and institutional invest-ment in the notion that reason and emotion are separate and irreconcilable and that, in a civilized society, rationality must prevail."[13] This is the tragically misguided notion that leads to the denial of children's rights and emotions.

———————————————

I hope I've made it clear that people learn best when they are emotionally involved with their learning, either because of keen interest and curiosity or because of a personal desire to solve a problem or master a skill. Ignoring this fundamental principle of learning leads to the educationist's futile struggle to motivate the passive pupil with rewards, good grades, and promises of *fun*.

It can also be said that negative emotions affect learning: boredom, fear, anxiety, disapproval, and shame can cause sti-fling aversions and phobias. The separation of intellect and

———————————————

[12] Alexander S. Neill, *The Free Child*, (London: Herbert Jenkins: 1953), 29.
[13] Stanley Greenspan, *The Growth of the Mind: And the Endangered Origins of Intelligence*, (Reading, MA: Addison Wesley: 1997), 2.

emotion, like the separation of mind and body, is a linguistic construct that leads us astray.

For the infant, sensorimotor experiences and emotion are directly associated, the most obvious being pleasurable feelings of warmth, touch, and fullness associated with sucking and feeding. These feelings promote a sense of well-being and confidence in the environment, making further forays and explorations possible, thereby enhancing the establishment of new and complex neural connections. Again, the converse is true if attunement between mother and child is not present and the environment is confusing, cold, or hostile. As Greenspan explains: "Human beings start to couple phenomena and feelings at the very beginning of life. Even infants only days old react to sensations emotionally, preferring the sound or smell of Mother, for example, to all other voices or scents."[14]

Babies as young as five to twelve weeks have unsuspected perceptual and intellectual abilities. Using special devices to measure gaze patterns and rates of sucking, researchers have found that very young infants become bored with repetition and then respond favourably to novel pictures or sounds, distinguish human speech sounds from other sounds, and clearly recognize the mother's face. Even newborns can distinguish between a song sung by the mother during pregnancy from a song they had not heard before. The same is true of hearing the mother's voice reading a story. To put it simply, babies are a lot smarter than we might think they are.

A conclusion we can draw is that a rich emotional life, based on positive and loving interaction with caregivers, before and after birth, is necessary to the ability to form abstract concepts and manipulate symbols. Additionally, it should be noted that an environment rich in objects such as toys,

---

[14] Greenspan, *The Growth of the Mind,* 18-19.

books, music, and child-proof household equipment provides a welcoming and stimulating atmosphere for the young explorer. The key here is "household equipment," in other words objects, including books, toys, and music that are part of the regular configuration of a household. It is not productive but indeed counterproductive to bring in objects that do not relate to everyday life. Specially designed "educational" toys and videos are not to be used as substitutes for genuine and warm human contact.

With this in mind, the reader will understand my disdain for the plastic gewgaws and cartoon videos that are marketed as stimulants to learning. If we look at these products as representative of culture, we must ask ourselves what is the culture to which we are introducing our children?[15]

How Children Learn

Another approach to the understanding of learning and growth does not rely on research or clinical experience but draws conclusions from direct interaction and play with children as well as intuitive understanding of their mental processes. John Holt (1923-1985), in his 1967 book, *How Children Learn*, made this position clear at the outset:

> This book is more concerned with describing effective learning than explaining it, or giving a theory about it. . . . What teachers and learners need to know is what we have known for some time: first, that vivid, vital, pleasurable experiences are the easiest to remember, and secondly, that memory works best when it is unforced, that it is not a

---

[15] I have written extensively about entertainment for children and supposed stimulants to learning. See "Learning as Fun or The Erosion of Childhood." *School and the End of Intelligence*, pp. 73-112.

mule that can be made to walk by beating it. . . . This book is more about children than about child psychology.[16]

Of course, in spite of what he says about not theorizing, he has clearly presented his theory of learning in these few sentences. Holt then goes on to decry laboratory research into brain function and learning:

> Making judgments about how the mind or the brain (they're not the same) works on the basis of a few (or even sixty-four) squiggles on a chart is like deciding what lives in the ocean by lowering and then pulling up a five-gallon bucket and seeing what you can find in it.[17]

John Holt was an ex-teacher whose two books *How Children Fail* and *How Children Learn* made an important contribution to educational thought in the 1960s. He then wrote seven other books, including *Teach Your Own*, espousing home schooling. In 1977 he began *Growing Without Schooling*, a bimonthly magazine devoted to promoting home schooling. Though publication terminated in 2001, a complete collection, in three volumes, is available from online booksellers.[18]

Holt concludes that most children's learning follows a trial and error method and that children naturally want to learn about the world around them. "A child has no stronger desire," he writes, "than to make sense of the world, to move freely in it, to do the things that he sees bigger people doing."[19] As Vygotsky's studies confirmed, younger children see

---

[16] John Holt, *How Children Learn, rev. ed.*. (New York, Delacorte Press: 1967) x-xi

[17] Holt, *How Children Learn*, 8.

[18] "A YouTube channel, *Growing Without Schooling* (GWS) features video and audio documents about learning outside of school, home chooling, self-directed learning, and the work of John Holt (1923-1985)." https://www.youtube.com/@Johnholtgws/featured

[19] Holt, *How Children Learn*, 32.

some activity or operation, then perform it, then compare what they are doing to the model, then revise their performance, compare, revise, etc. Isn't this what James, Tommy and Bobby, and Miles were doing? Then, as children grow older and develop the ability to manipulate linguistic symbols, they first form a verbal or symbolic notion of an action, then perform, then revise, etc. It's not hard to see how jumping in to "teach" the child something would interfere with the natural process of discovery and learning.

Language develops from signal to symbol. That is, words are first used to name things and to cause actions to happen: "Milk!" "No bed!" "Want choo-choo!" (A phenomenon familiar to any parent of a two-year-old.) At this stage words are firmly rooted to objects and actions. It is only later that words are used as symbols to create flexible sequences leading to thinking about concepts and planning action. The infant will first explore an object with his or her mouth, seeing how it will fit, how it tastes and feels. The young child seizes the toy and starts pushing and pulling to see what can be done with it, how to make it "go." The older child will look at the toy, perhaps even follow complicated instructions, and form mental images of what use it might be put to. In all cases, however, the activity will involve self-directed experimentation, trial and error, and revision.

No doubt there is nothing in Holt's observations and conclusions that would be objected to by Vygotsky. Nor would Vygotsky have disagreed with Caroline Pratt (1867-1954), also an ex-public school teacher who left the system in order to establish a school upon principles in which she believed. She was a contemporary of John Dewey (1859-1952) and, like him, believed that children have a natural desire to learn which is best served by engaging in real work out of which, without a pre-determined and fixed curriculum, they would acquire traditional school skills such as reading and arithmetic.[20] Pratt also espoused trial and error as the natural and most efficient manner in which children explored and learned about their world. Like John Holt and many others, most notably perhaps A.S. Neill, she believed that learning was as natural to children as growth, and that like a growing plant, this growth requires nurturing surroundings and conditions in order to flourish. In her own words:

> What I did have was a deep conviction, unspoken, indeed unconscious until much later, that a desire to learn was as natural and inevitable in children as the desire to walk in babies.
> How could anyone doubt that it was? Once beyond the eating-sleeping stage, every day, every hour of a young child's waking life is devoted to adventure, exploration, discovery of the world around him. . . . His greatest frustrations, aside from his own limitations, are the restrictions placed upon him by the adult world in his effort to touch, to feel, to see and smell and taste. And his method of learning? The first and best one, the one used by Neanderthal man and by the atomic scientist—trial and error.[21]

Another ex-teacher, at least an ex-traditional-school teacher, Alexander S. Neill (1883-1973) founded his Summerhill School in 1924, based on principles influenced by the thinking of Homer Lane, Wilhelm Reich, and perhaps even J. J. Rousseau. Neill believed that freedom from constraint and direction in an atmosphere of mutual respect in which children and adults had equal rights to run their own lives would nurture maximum intellectual growth and learning. "I hold

---

[20] This is exactly what was proposed and implemented by Johann Heinrich Pestalozzi as early as 1801. See *School and the End of Intelligence*, pp. 180-198, for a full description of Pestalozzi and his methods.
[21] Caroline Pratt, *I Learn from Children*. (New York: Cornerstone Library Publications, 1948), 14-15.

that education," he wrote in 1966, "should concern itself with the emotions and leave the intellect to look after itself"[22]

Among the more recent theorists on the subject of learning, Frank Smith contrasts what he calls the "classic view of learning" with the approach taken by school, which he calls the "official theory of learning". Classic learning is that kind of learning which takes place throughout early childhood. Essentially, as Smith often repeats, "You learn from the company you keep." So, children learn to talk by being with people who talk; they learn to read by having friends and family who read; they learn about numbers from people who work and play with numbers. This kind of learning is both effortless and permanent. Smith distinguishes between short-term memory, which has only to do with temporary electrical circuitry, and long-term memory, or learning, which affects the actual structure of the brain and determines who we are.

In contrast, the official theory of learning says that learning is hard and requires careful organization. This kind of learning is directed by experts who have compartmentalized the process into subjects, grades, levels, etc. The problem, as stated by David Cayley on the CBC program *Ideas* is that:

> What kids are learning, when they aren't learning their lessons, Smith says, are attitudes to themselves and to the subjects they're being taught. The reason, he thinks, is that we learn not as a task but by identification. We learn what fits our sense of who we are and who we want to be.[23]

Two aspects of Smith's theory of learning are: You learn from the company you keep and You learn what makes sense. "The company you keep" doesn't mean just the people in

---

[22] Alexander S. Neill, *"Neill, Neill, OrangePeel!" An autobiography by A.S. Neill*, (New York: Hart Publishing Company, Inc, 1972), 485.
[23] Canadian Broadcasting Corporation, *The Education Debates*, (Toronto: CBC Ideas Transcripts, 1998), 98.

whose presence you spend the most time. We learn from people we identify with, people we would like to be like. They could well be authors, musicians, or media personalities. It is through this learning from other people that we become who we are:

> Remember, we don't always learn what is best for us to learn, and it's not possible to forget something deliberately once we've learned it, especially when it is something about ourselves, about our identity. If we have learned that we can't do certain things, that we are not a certain kind of person, then we won't succeed no matter how much energy we expend or how much other people exhort us. We need therapy.
> I'm not being facetious. We're talking about changing the ingrained self-image of a person, and that is not accomplished through slogans, desire, reason, or even common sense.[24]

Another influential writer of the 1970s, James Herndon, described this kind of learning in his usual disarming way:

> Is there any man or woman on earth who knows how to read who doesn't feel quite capable of teaching his own child or children to read? Doesn't every father feel confident that his boy will come into the bathroom every morning to stand around and watch while the father shaves and play number games with the father and learn about numbers and shaving at the same time. . . . Want to know about Egypt? Mother or father or older brother or uncle or someone and the kid go down to the public library and get out a book on Egypt and the kid reads it and perhaps the uncle reads it too, and while they are shaving they may talk about Egypt.[25]

---

[24] Smith, *The Book of Learning and Forgetting*, 36.
[25] James Herndon, *How to Survive in Your Native Land.* (New York: Simon and Schuster, 1971), 106.

According to this approach, learning works best when it's based on human relations and mutual interests. Vygotsky would agree.

The other important aspect of learning as described by Smith is that of understanding. He claims that we simply can't learn anything that doesn't make sense to us. When James works the computer, for example, he uses it in a way that makes sense to him. To attempt to teach him the "proper" use of the computer would only be to confuse him and discount his own enthusiastic approach to the machine.

But learning does not have to be focussed on a particular subject or piece of equipment. Children are keen observers, able to size up a situation or a person and figure out, based on their knowledge and experience, how to deal with it. In other words, learning goes on continuously:

> We are learning all the time—about the world and about ourselves. We learn without effort every moment of the day. We learn what is interesting to us . . . and we learn from what makes sense to us (because there is nothing to learn from what confuses us except that it is confusing).[26]

This view of learning affirms what was said earlier about the process of learning when interest and curiosity are present. Like growth, learning is a natural process that will take place under almost any conditions, but with proper nourishment and congenial surroundings an organism will flourish.

Finally, learning only what makes sense to us means learning only what interests us. A friend of mine once said, "Children have no unanswered questions." What she meant by this was that if something a child sees does not make sense, the child will make up an explanation based on his or her limited experience. I remember, even now with a sense of

---

[26] Smith, *Book of Learning and Forgetting*, 31.

anger and humiliation, being faced, at age eight or nine, with long columns of addition or impossibly complicated long division problems that never came out even. I'm sure I was supposed to think, "Oh, lucky me, I get to perfect my arithmetic skills with these challenging problems!" Hardly. I asked myself "Why do I have to suffer?" What I decided was that there was a man somewhere, the one who was responsible for this workbook, who deliberately made up these exercises just to torment *me*. I was sure that he was somewhere, gloating maliciously over my misery. What I learned about arithmetic was that it was impossibly difficult. I was defeated.

By way of contrast, a few years earlier, when I was six or seven years old, I was fascinated by trains. We lived, at that time, across the road from the main train tracks leading out of Portland, Oregon. I kept a large scrapbook into which I pasted pictures of trains I had cut from newspapers and magazines. I studied the railroad timetables my father had brought home for me. I knew what the different engines were called, I knew where the trains that passed our house were going and when they'd get there, and I knew the difference between steam and diesel engines. From my work with trains, I learned about schedules, distances, speed, and that there were far-off places called New York, Chicago, and Omaha. What I learned in school was that I hated arithmetic and that it was too hard for me. Trains made sense to me, workbooks full of complicated numbers did not.

Frank Smith asks, "Why do [we] focus so much on what students fail to learn, rather than on what they are learning in its place, which may have much more significance in the students' lives?" Or as he put it in a radio interview:

> The point is we don't learn what we are expected to learn. People think that we will learn all matters of facts and particular skills in particular areas, abilities like reading and

writing and the rest of it. **In fact, what kids learn are attitudes towards these things and attitudes towards themselves.**[27] [emphasis added]

Intelligence

Intelligence, like "mind" or even "soul", is an elusive concept. It has yet to be seen, weighed, dissected, or measured. Well, whether or not it can be measured would be debated by those who espouse intelligence, or IQ, testing. To the popular mind, intelligence is manifested by displays of memory. If you can answer all the questions on *Jeopardy*, you must be pretty intelligent. To other people it's the application of school learning to everyday problems. If you can figure out how to make one-third of a cake by dividing fractions, or if you can convert grams to ounces at the butcher's counter, you must be pretty bright.

Let's go back for a moment, though, to James and Miles and Bobby and Tommy. Are these intelligent children? The assertion here is that, yes, they are, because in each case a learning or experiential problem was approached, dealt with, and solved in a creative and appropriate manner. James effectively and competently answered the question, "How can a three-year-old make use of a computer?" Clearly, its word-processing capabilities are neither of use nor of interest to him, what he cares about is how to make it do something, and he experiments at his own speed and in accordance with his physical abilities. There is no doubt in my mind that as he grows and continues to experiment with the computer, he will begin to discover *entirely on his own* many other things he can do with it.

---

[27] Canadian Broadcasting Corporation, *The Education Debates*, 98

Two-year-old Miles put his mind to solving his problem of access with stunning effectiveness. The set of nesting boxes was, no doubt, intended to "teach" seriation to a small child. (The boxes were also decorated with letters of the alphabet and animal pictures.) Again, the intended use of the implement was of little or no interest to him. He approached the problem laterally, sized up the possibilities, and, *voila!*, his parents now had a two-year-old operating the kitchen stove.

Bobby and Tommy were faced with three objects: a horizontal metal tank, a can of rainwater, and several paintbrushes. The three objects were quickly assembled into one action: that of painting. The use of a paintbrush for painting would appear inevitable to an adult or older child, just as the computer would suggest word-processing or Internet access, but to a four-year-old the world is still full of strange and interesting things that have no known, or even obvious, uses. To combine the three objects in question into one unified action is no less brilliant than the man who turned an ineffective new adhesive into Post-It Notes. The fact that the water on the galvanized surface of the water tank provided satisfying evidence of the progress and accuracy of the work of the young painters shows intelligent use of sharply perceived possibilities existing in found objects.

The point of these three examples is to show that intelligence cannot be measured by "how much you know" or even how well you can do on the Stanford-Binet test; no, it's more like how can you take what you have and make something out of it. Stanley Greenspan put it in these words:

> Intellectual capacity is more than mastery of impersonal cognitive tasks—puzzles, math problems, memory or motor exercises—or analytical thinking. . . . Intelligence represents two interrelated capacities: the ability to generate in-

tentions and ideas, and the ability to put these creations into a logical or analytical framework.[28]

It's important to note that creativity or "generating intentions" comes before logic and analysis. Intelligence involves passion, curiosity, and self-interest, qualities possessed by ingenuous two-year-olds as well as by knowledgeable and experienced (ahem) ninety-two-year-olds. These are attributes that cannot be measured by tests.

Robert Sternberg, a psychologist and psychometrician, defined three kinds of intelligence—analytic, creative, and practical—that make up what he calls "successful intelligence."

> The three aspects of successful intelligence are related. Analytical thinking is required to solve problems and to judge the quality of ideas. Creative intelligence is required to formulate good problems and ideas in the first place. Practical intelligence is needed to use the ideas and their analysis in an effective way in one's everyday life.[29]

Exactly how our young workers analyzed and solved the problems before them!

Work and Play

The observers and writers cited above would all seem to agree that children have an innate and powerful drive to grow and to learn. Most would also agree that emotion plays an important part in the wiring of brain circuitry in the first ten

---

[28] Greenspan, *The Growth of the Mind*, 125.
[29] Robert J. Sternberg, *Successful Intelligence: How Practical and Creative Intelligence Determine Success in Life*, (New York: Simon & Schuster, 1996), 127-128.

years of life. (Which is not to say that emotional involvement ceases to be important to effective learning in later life.)

Children's play is children's work. The work they do in manipulating and participating in their surroundings is as effortful and significant as any work performed by adults. Just because children are mostly inexperienced novices when it comes to using machinery, words, and tools, does not mean that their actions are not real. Immature logic is logic nevertheless. As Margaret Boden says, "Just as the newborn's grasping is real grasping, and a worm is a real, though lowly, living creature, so pre-operational thinking is in no way irrational, despite its logical immaturity."[30]

Children learn by acting, by mucking about, getting their hands dirty, by trial and error. They are likely to jump right in and start doing things, making things "go" before well-meaning adults have had a chance to "teach" them how it should be done. What is known as "the teachable moment" is a way for grownups to interfere with a child's learning. Children do not perceive a need to be told how to do things. As we saw with Bobby, James, Miles, and Tommy, children are keen observers and they are quick to say, "Me do it!"

You will see how this applies to our school that is good for kids.

Play, Play, Play

Our society often takes the moralistic view that play is a waste of time, and that life, especially the life of children, must be structured around a set of rules and expectations that are then to be enforced by discipline. It is thought that children won't learn anything unless they are taught and directed

---

[30] Boden, *Piaget*, 43.

by grownups in a structured setting. Unsupervised play is forbidden except under very limited conditions, usually on concrete surfaces and metal structures. Certain games are allowed as long as they can be labelled "sports" and are age-determined and highly competitive. These, too, are to be "coached" by adults and cheered on by parents and teachers. None of this can truly be called play.

In his 2013 book *Free to Learn*, Peter Gray, a professor in the Department of Psychology at Boston College, emphasizes the importance of play in social and mental development:

> Playing with other children, away from adults, is how children learn to make their own decisions, control their emotions and impulses, see from others' perspectives, negotiate differences with others, and make friends. In short, play is how children learn to take control of their lives.[31]

Genuine play, not under the control of authority, is where children learn to discipline themselves and operate within a social group. Peter Gray puts it this way:

> Self-education through play and exploration requires an enormous amount of unscheduled time—time to do whatever one wants to do without pressure, judgment, or intrusion from authority figures. That time is needed to make friends, play with ideas and materials, experience and overcome boredom, learn from one's own mistakes, and develop passions.[32]

I can hear the cries of horror over "unscheduled time—time to do whatever one wants" and "without judgment or intrusion from authority figures." This from those who be-

---

[31] Peter Gray, *Free to Learn, Why Unleashing the Instinct to Play Will Make Our Children Happier, More Self-Reliant, and Better Students for Life*, (New York: Basic Books, 2013), 157.
[32] Gray, *Free to Learn*, 100.

lieve that children must always be watched and told what to do and what not to do. They believe that education and learning must be directed and controlled. However, like so much of what passes as "common sense"—or more accurately "common nonsense"—this is exactly opposite to what nature determines and what is most efficient and productive.

The psychologist Lev Vygotsky, whom we met earlier, wrote, "The influence of play in a child's development is enormous."[33] He devoted a great deal of study to observing children at play, and drawing sometimes unexpected conclusions. Play, he believed, is always based upon its own rules and structure. For example, when a child plays mother or father to a doll, the observed behaviours of mothers and fathers form the rules by which the game is played. If you remember ever playing cops and robbers you'll know what he meant. Play then becomes the child's way of developing experience of the world and of learning to operate within a structured setting, however imaginary it might be. I refer back to the stories of our four young workers. I can't emphasize enough that all play is really children's work. And the work is devoted to the development of self-control, curiosity, and intelligence.

It is easy to see how early contact with screen images interferes with the natural process of learning. Schools and parents who supply young children with tablets or laptops, thinking that there is some advantage to early acquaintance with technology, are hampering if not destroying a child's natural drive to learn by association with other living human beings.

---

[33] Lev Vygotsky, *Mind in Society, The Development of Higher Psychological Processes*, ed. **Michael Cole, Vera** John Steiner, Sylvia Scribner, Ellen Souberman, (Cambridge, MA: Harvard University Press, 1978), 96.

THE DIGITAL REVOLUTION

Not all change constitutes progress. Just because some-thing can be done does not mean it should be done.-- UNESCO report "Technology in Educa-tion:"[34]

I wonder if it would have made a difference if, in 1908 when the number of cars first surpassed that of horses in New York City, if someone had said, "If we keep going at this rate and everyone drives a car, we will pave over our best farm land, pollute the atmosphere with exhaust fumes, and transform the shape of cities and countryside irrevocably and forever." Would it have made any difference?

In the same way, computers that seemed to hold so much promise in the 1950s have, in many ways, turned out to be a curse and blight on civilized culture. Through the analysis of ratings, computers now control how political campaigns are run, what entertainment will be available to us, how we do our banking, what products will be stocked in the supermar-ket, even how we access medical information. No one, least of all me, could have realized how social media and video games would come to dominate the lives of young people and adults. I don't think we have yet comprehended the profound effects this is having on the way we get information (or disin-formation), communicate with each other, and view the world. More significant is the way digital technology is re-shaping the human brain.

The computer and its numerous digital relatives totally change our way of being in the world, our way of relating to

---

[34] UNESCO, *Technology in Education: A Tool on Whose Terms*, Glob-al Education Monitoring Report 2023, 24

other people and of perceiving ourselves. This is a change in Western civilization paralleled only by the introduction of the printing press in the 15th century. The printing press not only offered access to unlimited amounts of information and an unheard of variety of ways of thinking to the vast majority of the populace, but it also established many of the concepts that we now accept as common sense: orderly progression from left to right, the use of print to disseminate information, persuasion, and entertainment, and the division of knowledge into chapters. But let's not kid ourselves, the computer screen is not just a slick way to get information as if it were some kind of new version of paper with print or pictures on it, it is something else altogether. Who is not familiar with the way the screen almost demands that we skip from one image to another, fall for "click bait," or tire of any program that lasts for more than a few seconds. As I will repeatedly point out, the computer screen is reshaping the human brain.

Small children are most profoundly affected by watching screen images, especially the highly-stimulating cartoons that are promoted as educational. In a TED Talk of 2011, [35] Dr. Dimitri Christakis, director of Seattle Children's Research Institute's Center for Child Health, Behavior and Development, a professor of pediatrics at the University of Washington School of Medicine, and a pediatrician at Seattle Children's Hospital, tells us that, "We are technologizing childhood today in a way that is unprecedented." He then offers two contrasting scenarios:

---

[35] Dimitri Christakis, "Media and Children," YouTube video, 0:16:11, December 28, 2011,
https://www.youtube.com/watch?v=BoT7qH_uVNo&ab_channel=TEDxTalks.

<u>One:</u> Children who have been read to, played with, sung to, and taken to museums and cultural events are never short of attention span. You might say that they are interested in everything.

<u>Two:</u> Sadly, the same is not true about children who have grown up with the constant stimulation of videos, cartoons, and children's entertainment. There you have the recipe for inattention and lack of curiosity.

As he explains, there are two types of stimulation. The one necessarily involves contact and communication with other people, and the other means growing up in a world of idiotic cartoon characters, constantly changing images, and the hypnotic quality of the ever-present screen. Especially enlightening is Dr. Christakis's comparison, in his TED talk, of two children's videos. The first, from *The Powerpuff Girls Movie*, is a fast action cartoon with rapid changing images and sudden loud noises. It is followed by a clip from *Mister Rogers' Neighbourhood*. You can hear the sigh of relief from the audience as they see Fred Rogers calmly looking directly at the camera (at you), as he explains the protocol of visiting a restaurant. The effect on attention hardly needs elaboration.

In another TED talk, Dr. Christakis, pointed out the significant impact of television watching on young children and future issues of attention span. In 1970, children started to watch television at age four, but by 2011 even babies of four months were watching up to four and half hours per day. They may be seeing regular television programing or videos made especially for children, but the results were the same: "Prolonged exposure to rapid image change during a critical period of brain development preconditions the mind to expect high levels of stimulation leading to inattention in later life."[36] *The longer the screen-watching time, the shorter the attention span.*

I once heard a young father say, "The way to keep kids quiet—cartoons!" The television or video screen provides a quick way for busy parents to avoid connecting with their kids, guaranteeing that the screen-addicted toddler will turn into the smartphone, video game, and social media addicted teenager.

Functioning in a democratic society suggests the ability to listen to others, to weigh ideas and opinions, and to arrive at conclusions based on co-operation with others. Would we ever learn this from *Sesame Street* or *Sponge Bob Square Pants?*

On the subject of an undreamed-of range of topics, one of the most exciting, to some, and frightening, to others, is the difficulty, if not impossibility, of censoring what goes out and comes in on the Internet. The amount of digital information flowing around the world is so vast that it is inconceivable to figure out a way to monitor it. No sooner is one objectionable website discovered and shut down than ten new ones on the same topic spring up. Parent's may install "web nannies" to filter what comes into their children's computers, but who knows whether the neighbours or the web cafes have similar controls, not to mention the fact that any smart kid can probably disable whatever programs are designed to limit his or her browsing.

The volume of material on sex available to titillate Internet users of any taste is legendary and speaks to a new and

---

[36] Dimitri Christakis, "Media and Children," TEDx Talks, Dec. 29, 2011, YouTube Video, 16:11,
https://www.google.com/search?client=firefox-b-
d&q=Dimitri+Christakis#fpstate=ive&vld=cid:699c0c49,vid:BoT7qH_
uVNo

unprecedented liberation in people's ability and willingness to communicate secret and previously suppressed longings. The implications of so-called cybersex are barely imaginable. Unlike books, which can be seized at borders or at point of sale, the Internet flows freely through wire, microfibre, and the airwaves of the "wireless world." Web sites are created and posted by individuals of whatever stripe wherever they may be. If we no longer have parents, grandparents, or church authorities to set and guide our morals and monitor our access to information, what might happen as we are barraged with innumerable concepts, ideas, and "alternate facts" is anybody's guess.

The individuals of whatever stripe, including you and me, who populate the Internet are, or can be, totally anonymous. In other words, that e-mail that you received could be from anyone anywhere, and the other people in the chat room or posting on the news group are probably completely unknown to you. Not only do you not know for sure who they are, but you also don't know where they are. The middle-aged pedophile posing as a teenager in a chat group has already become the bogeyman of the early twenty-first century. And while there is unquestionably an enormous amount of valuable and responsible information and opinion accessible on the net, there is an equal amount of misinformation and bigotry. It's true that you can access the Library of Congress or tour the Louvre Museum, but you can also find out how to make pipe bombs or learn that Jews are plotting to take over the world.

For a society that has been accustomed to having its standards set by authority of however dubious integrity, the Internet presents revolutionary and perplexing problems. If, in fact, we are unable to control what information and communication people, and especially our young people, have access to, what possibility do we have of creating a just and prudent society? Or is technology simply taking on a life of its own and developing in its own way out of our control. Is it a wonder that authority figures like teachers are losing control as they hand over digital devices to school children of even the tenderest age.

But that's not all. At the present time, developments in artificial intelligence are causing quite a flap, especially in the field of education. With good reason should they be worried. ChatGPT, as an example, can create real-sounding news releases, images, scholarly essays, or music as composed and performed by living or dead musicians. Remember though that these technologies are limited to information gathered and massaged from the web; they lack genuine intelligence, curiosity, feelings, and original humour. But don't breathe a sigh of relief; who knows what's in store. Technological developments seem, well *are*, limitless, for better or for worse.

Don't get me wrong, I am as amazed and impressed as anybody by what can be done, and there is no question that anything that a computer can do can be put to good use if used with intelligent discrimination. The trouble is that "intelligent discrimination" is rare. Like any number of good and useful things, like automobiles, television, or supermarkets, the marvel of their capabilities soon overwhelms any sense of moderation or evaluation of the consequences of overuse.

Computers and School, The Darker Side

Like the programmed learning of the 1950s and 60s, educators were quick to see that computers could provide a new, standardized, and exceedingly efficient means of instruction. As early as the 1970s, school people were believing that it was their duty to prepare kids for the digitized world of the future. Familiarity with all aspects of computer technology would, they said, lead to better and more profitable jobs. The goal had to be to supply every child in the school with a lap-top or similar computer. Lessons could be individualized, re-search would be a breeze, students could interact with one another, and tests could be administered and marked right on the spot. This had B. F. Skinner's *Teaching Box* beat hands down. Schools were quick to jump on the Apple or Microsoft bandwagon.

But surely the educationists are living in a dream world if they think that giving kids computers will lead them to the intense pursuit of academic achievement. They are ignoring the lure and attraction of the device itself. Yes, a computer makes possible access to a universe of information of all kinds, but the way in which that universe is accessed is set by the device itself. Anyone who uses the Internet for research will confirm how quickly one can be led astray. The tempta-tion to follow that suggested link (click bait), to check e-mail just one more time, or to be sure I'm not missing something on Facebook or TicTok, will slow down any progress on gaining or using serious knowledge or thought. The person who said that the Internet offers us information but no knowledge had the right idea, but maybe it is even better at offering brief bits of entertainment that are adapted to de-creasing attention spans. Now are we going to expect seven and eight-year-olds to avoid these temptations and stick to their lessons?

It is already known that attention spans, especially in young people, are getting shorter all the time. This becomes clear when we re-examine the ideas presented earlier about highly stimulating videos for very young children.

It was, and still is, felt that every school should have computers in it and be connected to the "wired world." The question is, do we use the computer as a clever new teaching tool to promote the same message that school has had since, well, probably around 1750, or do we investigate and explore the new technology to see what it can do for us? Neil Postman has made a similar statement:

> What we need to consider about the computer has nothing to do with its efficiency as a teaching tool. We need to know in what ways it is altering our conception of learning, and how, in conjunction with television, it undermines the old idea of school.[37]

Teachers will often try to make use of *fun* as a way of luring kids into things like reading and arithmetic, even history and literature. Do we really want to degrade the importance of learning by disguising it as some kind of game or contest? What was once learned at grandfather's knee as he read from the *King James Bible* or on mother's lap as she paged through a picture book engaging even the youngest child in conversation is now to be gleaned from goofy videos or some amusing classroom entertainment.

> Without getting too far off the track here, I invite you to look at a couple of "educational" YouTube videos. First, the wide-grinning, ever-so-cute Ms. Rachel and her *Toddler Learning Videos*[38] designed for the edification of preschoolers (guaranteed to turn them off any kind of learning forever). Or, for the more serious minded, *SciShow Kids*.[39] This highly-rated YouTube channel offers

[37] Postman, *Technopoly*. 19.
[38] Ms Rachel - Toddler Learning Videos; Learn About Emotions and Feelings with Ms Rachel | Kids Videos | Preschool Learning Videos | Toddler. **Copy and paste: rb.gy/rhrzbs**
[39] SciShow Kids: https://www.youtube.com/user/scishowkids

dozens of "science" videos presented by the ever-cheerful hosts accompanied by their robot mouse named, you guessed it, *Squeeky*. I dare you to watch any one of these videos without cringing in revulsion or horror at the condescending, patronizing cuteness or *Gee whizz, Mr. Science!* chatter. Well, that is unless you are an over-stressed parent or teacher desperate to find some way to engage the distracted attentions of a four-year-old or a classroom full of digital-brained kids. Their attention will be grabbed by anything on a screen in preference to a live human speaking. Speaking of *Mr.Science*, I think it will do your brain good to hear Bob and Ray[40] as they take us to "the modern well-equipped laboratory" where little Jimmy Schwab is about to observe Mr. Science perform "one of his fascinating experiments." [41]

In spite of the obvious risks and disadvantages, schools have not hesitated to bring new technologies into the classroom. It seemed like such a good idea at first that the non-profit initiative *One Laptop per Child* was formed at the World Economic Forum in 2005. The plan was that a laptop computer could be bought by governments and distributed to children everywhere. The technology bandwagon proved irresistible, so millions of laptops were purchased and handed out to kids, who had no problem learning how to use them. In poorer countries where many were living on less than $2.00 per day, some wags even suggested that clean water, schools, and access to medical care might be of greater bene-

---

[40] Bob Elliott (1923-2016) and Ray Goulding (1922-1990) were a satirical comedy duo often poking fun at the very medium (radio) in which they were performing.

[41] Don't miss this wonderful spoof of science education by Bob and Ray. Copy and paste: rb.gy/p5yuxa

fit. As we have seen, though, the richer countries, not being held back by economic concerns, quickly equipped every school kid with a laptop and, before long, a smart phone.

For those less bedazzled by technological marvels, John Wood, founder of *Room to Read* (a non-profit that builds schools and libraries), pointed out that a $2,000 library can serve 400 children, costing just $5 a child to bring access to a wide range of books in the local languages and English; also, a $10,000 school can serve 400–500 children ($20–$25 a child). He suggested that these are more appropriate solutions for education in the dense forests of Vietnam or rural Cambodia.[42]

That brings us to the cellphone. I doubt that any other technology has grown and spread as widely or as fast. Since its introduction and the establishment of wireless cellular networks, in 1973, this technology has grown with blinding speed. After IBM brought in the smartphone, in 1992, there has been no looking back. The smartphone enables access to the Internet and hence to e-mail, texting, and social media at any and all times of the day or night This means that the owner of a phone need never be away from the worldwide web and all that that implies. For most people, and that is *most* people, the smartphone has replaced all other forms of communication, entertainment, and face-to-face talk. How often are we told of a group of people seated together in a restaurant all engaged in their phones and not talking to or looking at each other. Such "old-fashioned" practices as conversation or, heaven forbid!, letter writing have been dropped

---

[42] Lashinsky, Wood, et al, *Scaling Organizations Panel, Software Conference*, accessed September 28, 2023, http://web.archive.org/web/20130729205322id_/http://itc.conversations network.org/shows/detail1033.html.

in the dustbin along with family dinners, reading newspapers, and listening to classical music.

According to a report, in April 2022, by the website *Statista* [43] roughly forty per cent of kids age two to six, fifty per cent of kids age seven to eleven, and nearly ninety per cent of kids age twelve to seventeen had cellphones. (These figures apply to Canada.) Given the well-known addictive qualities of cellphone, especially smartphone, use, how are schools going to deal with kids who can't leave their phones alone? They are already sneaking peeks at un-school-approved websites on the laptops they were given, so why not on the easier-to-conceal phone? The lure of Instagram, TikTok, Snapchat, Facebook, YouTube, and the like quickly become irresistible, and kids are glued to their phones at every opportunity, even in the classroom whenever they can get away with it. Social media sites offer the never-ending promise of something new, different, or exciting. How are you going to tear your students away from that?

How about simply banning cellphones in school? Or at least in the classroom? At first, most schools did attempt to ban cellphone use during class or even anywhere in school. When this turned out to be impossible, they caved in and decided to navigate phone use toward educational purposes. After all, schools had jumped on the digital bandwagon with computer tablets for homework and class assignments since the early 2000s; only a few diehards mourned, or even noticed, the gradual abandoning of the written and printed word which had been the basis of education and learning for centuries. However, limiting cellphone use was problematic. It would seem puzzling to anyone who grew up in the pre-

---

[43] "Mobile phone usage among children and teens in Canada as of April 2022, by age group," accessed September 19, 2023, https://www.statista.com/statistics/1319950/canada-mobile-usage-kids-and-teens-by-age/.

cellphone days that some parents objected to even a partial ban because they were afraid of losing touch with their kids. "All too often, principals are afraid to crack down. They bend to the strident minority of parents who insist on their kids' inviolable right to carry phones—which generally translates as their own need to be in constant touch with their kids."[44] Since it was proving impossible to get rid of phones, why not use them for learning as sort of enhanced laptop computers?

An extensive report on technology in education by UNESCO, while not calling for, as some reports have it, a complete ban on cellphones in schools, emphasizes the importance of human face-to-face interaction in education and a cautionary approach to the use of technology, especially cellphones, in classrooms.

> Technology should not be viewed as the solution, but as a supportive tool in overcoming certain barriers to education access. The most effective interventions are those that put learners' interests as the focal point and support human interaction, making use of adequate in-person support, extensive teacher training and appropriate technology for the specific context. The best learning systems never rely on technology alone.[45]

In the rush to bring technology into the classroom, schools forgot to ask the basic question: How does extended time reading or writing on a screen affect the developing brain?[32] Also ignored were the broader implications of how technology affects the lives of children:

> Technology has fundamentally changed the way in which children exercise and realize their rights, including their rights to both education and privacy. While under certain

---

[44] Naomi Buck, "A Constant Distraction," *Globe and Mail*, September 2, 2023.
[45] UNESCO, *Technology in Education*, 42

conditions the use of technology in education can enhance children's opportunity to learn, it can also put their physical and mental integrity, privacy, and dignity at risk.[46]

The award-winning author and professor of reading Maryanne Wolf distinguished between the *reading brain* and the *digital brain*. Screen reading and print reading are not just two versions of the same thing, they differ to the extent that the chemistry of the brain itself is profoundly changed. This implies what amounts to a revolution in society, from people who are attentive, thoughtful, and curious, to people who can't pay attention to anything for more than a few seconds and are constantly in search of greater stimulation and diversion.

So how will we deal with computers and smartphones in our ideal school, the school that is good for kids? The basic idea of freedom is that people can do whatever they like as long as they don't interfere with the freedom of others. My belief is that children who are free to play as much as they like and with each other are unlikely to find screen-watching very appealing or interesting. Older kids will also find person-to-person banter, or simply hanging out with other kids, far more exciting than TikToc or Snapchat.

I think we can be sure that computer and cellphone use are issues that will arise frequently in meetings and in smaller groups. Learning about opinions of others and taking part in discussions of this kind can be a major part of learning and of growing up. It happens best in an atmosphere of freedom and approval.

---

[46] UNESCO, *Technology in Education*, 158

THE DISAPPEARING ADULT

Without a clear concept of what it means to be an adult, there can be no clear concept of what it means to be a child.—Neil Postman.[47]

If the sixteenth century saw the beginning of childhood as a social construct, the 21st century is seeing the end of it. In *Centuries of Childhood*,[48] Philippe Ariès pointed out that prior to the 16th century, young children were regarded as miniature adults and were fully involved in adult activities: work, sex, carousing, and punishment. According to Neil Postman, it was the dissemination of printed material that created a division between those who could read, adults, and those who couldn't, children. He further suggests that this established the so-called "age of reason" (seven years), since this is the age at which young people are able to demonstrate an ability to read. Of course, just being able to read was not enough. It was necessary to have read considerably in order to be knowledgeable and thoughtful enough to engage in public discourse.

The consequence of this division between young and old was, however, to create a new cohesion. Adults who knew how to read were able to provide for the young an entrée into the grown-up world. It fell upon parents and other family members to introduce children into reading in the same way that children were being introduced into the world of work. The distinction between childhood and adulthood meant that

---

[47] Neil Postman, *The Disappearance of Childhood*, (New York: Vintage Books, 1982), 98.
[48] Philippe Ariès, *Centuries of Childhood, A Social History of Family Life, trans Robert Baldick*, (New York: Vintage Books, 1962).

adults had achieved a level of knowledge and experience above that of children. Therefore, children were excluded from what were now regarded as exclusively adult activities: political discussion, voting, drinking, sex, attendance at serious theatrical or musical performances, driving cars, or sophisticated dining. Age twenty-one was established as the time when a person could be knowledgeable and thoughtful enough to participate in the adult world. Up until that time he was excluded from it. [49]

The Industrial Revolution and the 19th century saw not only the horrendous exploitation of child labour, especially in England, but also the subsequent sentimentalization of childhood as well as various movements leading to the protection of children. Children were now regarded as tender creatures in need of protection, nurture, and moral guidance. They were provided with clothing and playthings designed with children in mind. The 19th century also saw the widespread introduction of public schools and ultimately compulsory attendance. Well-minded people saw school as a way of getting seven-year-olds out of the mines and factories.

The introduction of compulsory public schooling in the mid-nineteenth century also created a division between generations in that instruction in various academic skills, whether they were needed or not, was now provided by adults who were relative strangers: teachers. School attendance kept young people out of their homes for the greater part of the day and out of the workplace completely. It was now expected that children would learn about professions and occupations, or what it meant to be an adult, by being told about them in school rather than by experiencing them first hand.

---

[49] But would the average twenty-one-year-old, having been excluded by school from adult society up to that time, be able to contribute in any constructive way to the grown-up world, especially to that of a democratic society?

They were now *subjected* to education with no say in how or what they were to learn.

Two catastrophic world wars dragged thousands of young North American men and women into devastating battle in foreign countries. Those who returned had experienced an otherwise not available exposure to other cultures as well as the sobering effects of witnessing the mass slaughter of comrades and enemies. Twentieth century technology meant that, in both world wars, troops, supplies, and ideas, could be transported around the world at previously unheard of speeds. The addition of radio and photography brought first-hand knowledge of war, again with unprecedented immediacy, to the general public. To the extent that people resisted governments' relentless propagandizing, they were able to question the reasons for wars and especially to question the need for going off to foreign countries to be killed or to kill other individuals for whom they had no particular personal animosity. In my opinion, these questions, however unstated they might be, were passed on to the generation following World War II and led directly to resistance to American participation in wars in Korea and Vietnam and the creation of the youth culture of the 1960s.

Popular Music and The Youth Market

But even before the 1960s, merchants of entertainment were discovering a large and previously unexploited youth market. The emergence, or rather explosion, onto the entertainment scene of Frank Sinatra in 1942 saw the creation of an audience made up almost exclusively of teenage children, especially girls. Technological advances in electro-acoustical recording meant that 10-inch 78 rpm records could be manufactured and sold at a price that teenagers could afford. Movies featuring teen idols were a gold mine just waiting to be exploited. While the sociological history of popular music and entertainment is an entire study to itself, suffice it to say that prior to Sinatra, with his boyish and fragile appeal, most musical entertainment was aimed at an adult audience, and popular singing artists like Bing Crosby, Rudy Vallee, Ella Fitzgerald, and Vera Lynn, had grownup, rather than childish, looks and appeal. It might be added that a significant aspect of Sinatra's attraction to the young audience was that many parents disapproved of the furor, amounting to a youth cult, around his popularity. A new market was ready to be exploited.

Though Sinatra's personal appeal was largely to the young, the music and lyrics that he sang were not much different from those of the entertainers who were still aiming at the adult audience. The romantic sentiments expressed in his songs belonged to a grown-up or at least young grownup realm, and the technical aspects of his vocalism—phrasing, voice production, interpretation—were in the finest traditions of the singers of popular ballads and musical comedy. As you read on, keep in mind that Sinatra and other singers of the time were accompanied by an orchestra of adult musicians. It wouldn't take long for that to change.

Also around this time something new and different was brewing in the American south among African-American musicians and singers. Growing out of New Orleans style jazz, the blues, boogie-woogie, and gospel, a new form was given the name, in 1947, *Rhythm and Blues*. It was marked by a strong, repetitious, and pervasive beat underlining an instrumental group consisting (usually) of horns and piano with an emotional vocal line expressing oppression and longing for freedom. This was the origin of what we now know as *Rock and Roll*. Though not originally aimed at a youth market, it soon became so when it was taken over, in the late 1950s, by groups of nice English white boys. Enter the Beatles, the Rolling Stones, Led Zeppelin, the Who, and many others soon to be emulated by aspiring young American bands.

The enormous popularity of Elvis Presley and later The Beatles was largely based on a youth market. The genesis of the style of popular music was no longer coming from the adult world of musical comedy and parlour ballads but from the rhythm, sexual energy, and rebellious sentiment of youth. This continued through the 1960s with the emergence of a powerful youth culture with its own music and political stance. The sentiment of the time was "Never trust anyone over thirty," and the music of such hit recording artists as Bob Dylan, The Beatles, The Rolling Stones, Led Zeppelin, and The Grateful Dead, virtually swept away any form of popular music based on traditional styles. It could be said that developments in popular music now began in the youth culture and filtered up to the grown-up market.

It is important to note that *Rock and Roll*—soon shortened to *Rock*—bands were made up of young, almost exclusively young, players, and almost always boys. The music was loud, very loud, rhythms were pounding and repetitious, instruments were limited to electric guitars and keyboard. Any vocal line was screamed into a microphone, only contributing to the overall powerful and driving sound. The spirit of the genre encouraged rebellion and challenge to authority, creating a platform for important social and political issues. Rock also influenced fashion in clothing. Individuality and rebellion could be expressed in the way young people dressed, breaking free from older social norms.

In a 2015 article in *The New Yorker*, Louis Menard expressed it thus:

> To this way of thinking, rock and roll—the music associated with performers like Chuck Berry, Little Richard, Bud-

71

dy Holly, and the early Beatles—is music that anyone can play (or can imagine playing) and everyone can dance to. The learning curve for performing the stuff is short; the learning curve for appreciating it is nonexistent. The instrumentation and the arrangements are usually simple: three or four instruments and, frequently, about the same number of chords. You can add horns and strings and backup singers, and you can add a lot more chords, but the important thing is the feeling. Rock and Roll feels uninhibited, spontaneous, and fun. There's no show-biz fakery coming between you and the music. As with any musical genre, it boils down to a certain sound. Coming up with that sound, the sound of unrehearsed exuberance, took a lot of work, a lot of rehearsing.[50]

By the 1980s, the in-your-face exuberance and creativity of Rock was dying out and being replaced by the more-or-less underground punk, grunge, and heavy metal. Even these were pushed out by the emergence of rap, another musical form that originated as Black social and political commentary. Rap was soon sanitized by white performers into a "daring" pseudo-poetical form, replete with the requisite obscenities.

By 1980, the rebellious youth of the 1960s were turning forty and older, leading to a new and reactionary conservative movement. Young people were now cautioned to stay in school, get good grades, proceed to university, etc., or else "You'll end up poor, on the streets and addicted to drugs." Even the casual observer can see how this divided society into the successful middle- and upper-middle classes from the reviled failures and dropouts. After all, "It's their own fault." And as expected, popular music now became ultraconservative in a bizarre manufactured kind of way. Rock and Roll

---

[50] Louis Menard, "The Elvic Oracle, Did anyone invent rock and roll?" (The New York, November 8, 2015)
https://www.newyorker.com/magazine/2015/11/16/the-elvic-oracle

was a matter of nostalgia and the memory of Woodstock would elicit only a few tut-tuts.

What started as the fabrication of here-today-gone-tomorrow highly profitable entertainers such as Britney Spears, The Spice Girls, and the Backstreet Boys, with their pseudo-innocent yet highly provocative sexuality, has been superseded by slicker and more visually appealing pop stars of the 2020s. While the most listened to and watched tend to be solo performers (with, of course, electronically generated backup) like Miley Cyrus, Katie Perry, Taylor Swift, and Justin Bieber. (You'll notice the predominance of female performers of, more or less, adult status.) Of course they must be young and sexy, making every effort to "sing" in a voice that sounds adolescent. Songs are more simple and repetitious than ever, consisting of a four- or eight-bar phrase, always in four-four metre, repeated for three to four minutes. Accompaniments sound amorphous, electronic, and unobtrusive. The "star" is now the main attraction, and people line up to pay thousands of dollars to attend a live concert performance. "Live" is merely nominative however, because electronic enhancement is there to deliver a loud and immediate sound with the lead singer glued to a hand-held microphone. Glitz and glamour predominate. A "concert" in this sense is not just someone on a stage delivering the songs they have become known for, it is a massive production involving a hundred or more dancers, backup singers, musicians, lighting and sound technicians, not to mention all the pre-performance publicity, box office (i.e. the enormously profit-making Ticketmaster), and elaborate travel arrangements. This is a far cry from the earlier times of a four-part rock band or solo artist with accompanist. And even farther from a time of grown-up performers and grown-up audiences.

Have a look at the way sung words have changed:

When the deep purple falls over sleepy garden walls
And the stars begin to twinkle in the night
In the mist of my memory, you wander on back to me
Breathing my name with a sigh.

In the still of the night once again I hold you tight
Though you've gone, your love lives on when moonlight
beams
And as long as my heart will beat, sweet lover, we'll
always meet
Here in my deep purple dreams.[51]

Love, love me do
You know I love you
I'll always be true
So please, love me do
Whoa, love me do
Someone to love
Somebody new
Someone to love
Someone like you.[52]

So long, Daisy May
I picked the petals, he loves me not
Something different bloomed, writing in my
room

---

[51] 1938, Peter DeRose and Michael Parish.
[52] 1962, Paul McCartney and John Lennon.

I play my songs in the parking lot
I'll run away

I called a taxi to take me there
I search the party of better bodies
Just to learn that my dreams aren't rare

You're on your own, kid
You always have been.[53]

Enough said. There can be no room for sophisticated poetry in a society devoted to being young.

The Disappearing Adult

What matters is that the youth market and the adult market have merged. There is no longer a distinction between youth and grown-up taste. Popular music is created with the youth market and the digital brain in mind. Keep it simple, keep it sexy, keep it short, and keep it loud.

Consequently, attendance at serious, non-commercial, musical performances like symphony and chamber music concerts, opera, and solo recitals is rapidly and drastically reducing, attended, as is often lamented, solely by the aging "blue-rinse" crowd. Developments in serious music composition and performance are totally ignored by the media while the latest pop stars are promoted relentlessly. There was a time, very much in my memory, when there were radio broadcasts of classical music like the Bell Telephone Hour, The Standard Hour, The Voice of Firestone, and numerous others. And, starting around 1930, live broadcasts from the

---

[53] 2022, Taylor Swift with Jack Antonoff.

75

Metropolitan Opera were heard every Saturday. The NBC (National Broadcasting Corporation) paid for a full symphony orchestra and a two-hour broadcast every Sunday just for the conductor Arturo Toscanini. This program often featured complete operas with a cast of great singers of the time. A lot of such programming was continued on to television (Ed Sullivan's show often featured opera singers) until it was driven out by the reliance on ratings. (Find out what they're watching and give them more of it.) So, the adult world of serious music was replaced by sit-coms, the latest pop hits, and a growing plethora of commercials. The same can be said of radio and television drama and enlightened news casts. All amounting to a deterioration and amalgamation of popular taste and a depletion of demands on focused attention. It is obvious that this trend is continuing, much to the benefit of advertising and commercial interests. "Keep 'em stupid, sell 'em more stuff." And don't get me started on sports.

Can our school-that-is-good-for-kids counter this trend and honour true adulthood, intelligent pursuit of learning, respect for the past, and unconditional positive regard for youth?

Media and Apparel

In earlier years parents shook their heads in wonder and disapproval at the tastes of their children, but now young people are regarding the adult world with disdain and distaste, while at the same time, many adults are adopting the ways and styles of their children. It is now not unusual to see grown men and women dressed in clothing previously deemed only appropriate for children at play. The clothing that used to belong to childhood—jeans, running shoes, tee shirts, baseball caps—have now become common dress for

76

adults, no matter what the occasion. Fitness clubs, cosmetics, and clothing are marketed to middle-aged adults with the promise of eternal youth.

Since the advent of television, and now of the Internet, the same entertainment and information are readily and equally available to children and adults. Accordingly, as the young people in our culture become more and more privy to aspects of the world that formerly belonged to adults, the grown-ups in our culture, desiring to be forever young, are abandoning the symbols and privileges of adulthood. As young people solidify a culture of their own that has become the upbeat, in the moment, lifestyle that everyone strives for, teachers and parents try to relate to the kids by being like them, adopting the same fashions, listening to the same music, and eating the same fast food.

In the same way that the distinction between childhood and adulthood was created by the printing press, the new media are obliterating it. As pointed out, children and adults now watch the same entertainment on television, have access via the Internet to the same information, and are considered equally as important as target markets by the purveyors of commercial products.

Small wonder, then, that children are not looking to parents and teachers as role models and sources of knowledge and wisdom. And because school, daycare, and a myriad of child-oriented sports and activities force children by segregation into a separate social group of their own, even dividing that group into smaller groups based on age and ability, a set of standards and mores have self-generated within those groups. Those standards and mores are more powerfully influenced by media and fashion than they are by the adults with whom the children have so little association. Because children, however bright and perceptive they may be, lack experience upon which to judge the value of behaviour, the culture of young people is usually based upon power and status, popularity and fashion, in short, conformity, forced or otherwise. Grown up people are looking to youth for models of speech, social activity, and political savvy.

Politics

Political discourse has deteriorated to the extent that political leaders are now judged on how good looking they are, how cute their kids are, how pretty their wives are, what evangelical denomination they ascribe to, and what catchy slogans they can harp on. The modern day politician has to pay careful attention to "image." It's best if he or she looks and acts like "just folks," and above all don't appear to be too intellectual. A brainy and thoughtful political leader is a no go. So, political debate focuses on name-calling and vituperative criticism. Content is reduced to wedge issues like abortion, immigration, and vaccination. These are issues on which the public is strongly divided into yes-or-no, us-against-them factions eliminating any possible mature discussion or weighing of significant issues.

There is plenty of evidence that political speeches are becoming shorter and simpler than those of the past. An article in *The Atlantic* informs us that "Presidential Speeches Were Once College-Level Rhetoric—Now They're for Sixth-Graders."[54] In other words, such speeches are designed to appeal to the lowest common denominator, and it's getting lower all the time. After all, the "wedge issues" do not lend themselves to detailed analysis. Mature and adult discussion

---

[54] Derek Thompson, "Presidential Speeches Were Once College-Level Rhetoric—Now They're for Sixth-Graders," (The Atlantic, Oct. 14, 2014), https://www.theatlantic.com/politics/archive/2014/10/have-presidential-speeches-gotten-less-sophisticated-over-time/381410/.

and examination of issues is no longer possible. In a fun-loving world, politicians have to behave like entertainers or, better still, combatants in a rhetorical wrestling match.

The School and the Grownup

Tales of bullying and violence in school are all too commonplace and horrific, though to this writer not surprising. As Frank Smith so ardently points out, "You learn from the company you keep," and if the company you keep consists of characters in television sitcoms, other inexperienced young people, ad men, YouTube stars, and adults whose main concern is control, you are left to put together a culture of your own—with dire results.

It would appear obvious, then, that in rethinking how we educate our children, our prime concern must be how we restructure the association between adults and young people. In a functioning school, adults and children are free to work together—or not—on various projects such as writing, reading, drawing, and discussing. What we know as authority must be based on learning and the wisdom of experience, not upon superior strength or titled position. Children must be able to see that adults struggle with problems, make mistakes, and experience frustration. And they must also be able to see that adults have something to say about the experience of learning and living. This can only happen in an atmosphere of individual rights and free association where every person of whatever age is treated with respect and not subjected to grading, judging, and direction from external sources. We're talking about a community—a society—in which people see each other as equals, each having thoughts and opinions that merit hearing and thoughtful consideration.

79

WHAT'S WRONG WITH SCHOOL

Ideally, schools exist to preserve and regenerate learning and the arts, to give children the tools with which they may create the future. At worst, they produce uniform, media-minded grown-ups to feed the marketplace with workers, with managers, and with consumers.—Stephen Nachmanovitch[55]

So far we have looked at a number of phenomena which affect the way in which we attempt to integrate children into our society and how these might change our thinking about learning and school. We are faced with revolutionary technology which not only changes the way in which we might learn but also changes the way in which people communicate and relate to each other. The almost universal attachment to screen media is, in fact, changing the structure of the human brain. Sweeping social changes, mostly the result of technology, are changing the way in which adults perceive children and children perceive adults. It is also changing the way people participate, or don't participate, in democratic society.

It is my opinion that our current approach to schooling is not recognizing the depth of cultural change taking place any more than it recognizes how learning takes place and intelligence develops. The school as we know it is, after all, based on a model developed in the eighteenth century. What follows is a look at some aspects of what we now think of as traditional education with an eye to seeing how they interfere with children's learning and undermine their curiosity, and intelligence.

---

[55] Stephen Nachmanovitch, *Free Play: Improvisation in life and art*, (New York: Tarcher/Putnam, 1990).

What I Learned

When I first started teaching, like most young teachers I thought that school was good and necessary for children. I believed that school was the place where they would acquire necessary skills like reading and using numbers, the necessities of adult life and work. But after a few months of exhorting the kids to pay attention, follow directions, and do their homework, I began to feel frustrated with the whole process. What were we actually doing here? Was all this really benefiting these kids? They didn't seem particularly interested in what we were doing.

I started to see that school was not about learning and teaching after all, it was about a power struggle. It was a battle between a handful of teachers and several hundred youngsters with the teachers having, or so they thought, the upper hand because they could deal out grades, punishments, and rewards. I say "or so they thought" because the youngsters would resort to subtle forms of resistance, such as failing to comprehend the simplest of concepts in arithmetic or grammar, suddenly having a broken pencil during some crucial bit of seat work, making up excuses for not doing required assignments, not being able to find a necessary textbook, daydreaming instead of hanging on teacher's every word, needing to go to the washroom at some key moment, and other endlessly creative subterfuges.

Even the kids who excelled at schoolwork seemed to do so mainly for the prize of a good report card, a pat on the back, and gold medal at the rewards ceremony.. They were very good at following directions and at doing what they were told. Their pleasure in learning what the school offered them was in the rewards they reaped for being model students, for knowing that they were better than the other kids. What would happen to those good students if you took away the top grades, the prizes, and pats on the back? Would they still pursue their studies—out of interest alone? Whatever the answers, most of the kids were *not* good students. They preferred to be messy, indifferent, inattentive, or rebellious. Their energies were devoted to a million small ways to frustrate and irritate the system. They didn't even pretend to be interested in what was being taught, just as long as they could do enough to get by.

The *good* teacher is good at what is known as "classroom management." If you can keep twenty-five or so rambunctious kids quiet and appearing to devote themselves to their studies, you must be a really good teacher and those kids must really be learning something. But what is that something?

So, What Is Going On?

In his book *Dumbing Us Down*, John Gatto, an award-winning teacher of twenty-six years' experience in Manhattan public schools, lists seven lessons that "are universally taught from Harlem to Hollywood Hills." [56] The seven lessons are: 1. Confusion; 2. Class Position; 3. Indifference; 4. Emotional Dependency; 5. Intellectual Dependency; 6. Provisional Self-Esteem; and 7. One Can't Hide. These make up what he calls, in the subtitle of his book: "The hidden curriculum of compulsory schooling."

The hidden curriculum lies in the way in which the school structures its activities. The curriculum is imposed from on

---

[56] John Taylor Gatto, *Dumbing Us Down: The Hidden Curriculum of Compulsory Schooling*. (Philadelphia: New Society Publishers, 1992), 1.

high without regard to how meaningful it might be in the lives of the students or the teachers. Time limits are set on everything. The day is divided into periods with each period devoted to a different and unrelated subject, so that no one interest can be worth pursuing, or as Gatto puts it, "Students never have a complete experience except on the installment plan."[57] Children are segregated by age and ability. Even within the age segregation ("unlike anything seen in the outside world"[58]) children are further divided arbitrarily into classes or divisions alienating them from the members of other classes with whom they are often placed in competition to see who is "better." Children learn to become dependent upon the approval or disapproval of authority. Some learn that success is gauged by the approval rating given by a teacher, while others reject approval and devote their energies to arousing anger and disapproval. You may be allowed certain privileges, but you have no rights. Since the school tells you what is worth learning, there is little point in developing interests and passions of your own. Those will not improve your grade point average. And finally, as Gatto points out, students are "under constant surveillance. There are no private spaces for children, there is no private time."[59] The final result is emphasis on conformity, mediocrity, timidity, and confusion, or to use Gatto's words, "dumbing down."

But surely the well-intentioned and well-trained people who are teachers and school administrators aren't diabolically plotting to undermine children's learning and destroy their good will and self-confidence. Most people in schools maintain a feeling of idealism and a genuine belief in the worth of what they are doing. They truly want to help children to

[57] Gatto, *Dumbing Us Down*, 6
[58] Gatto, *Dumbing Us Down*, 2
[59] Gatto, *Dumbing Us Down*, 11

achieve what they consider to be their best and to look forward to success in life. Unfortunately, however, they are caught in a set of unexamined beliefs and assumptions that turn their best intentions upside down. Most of these beliefs and assumptions are embodied in Gatto's Seven Lessons, resulting in "conformity, mediocrity, timidity, and confusion."

The School's Rules and Regulations

The school sets certain conditions which have been determined to be necessary for the school kind of learning to take place. Let's remember that the child who enters school has already acquired most of the skills, and much of the knowledge, needed to lead an effective life, all without structured teaching. The school now enters with its own expectations of what and how a person should learn. The school's rules and standards are often at odds with the child's own interests, curiosity, and personal needs. The school says, in effect, "We know what's good for you, you don't."

If the country's constitution guarantees certain individual rights and freedoms, these must be abandoned upon entering school, in the same way that rights and freedoms are forgone upon entering prison. First of all, as we have noted above, a child is deprived of any right to privacy. He or she is now part of a group of peers and not allowed rights of association outside of that group, except only at certain times and under very limited conditions. Nor is a child allowed solitude or privacy, except in some cases as a punishment, so-called "timeouts" which bear a chilling resemblance to those of prisons. And like prisoners, school children are deprived of freedom. Once enrolled in a school, a child may no longer come and go as he or she pleases nor respond to the exigencies of everyday life. Comings and goings are now determined by the school's agenda, its timetables, and its classrooms. Emphasis is placed upon punctuality and speed in responding to time constraints. You can't just walk away from school if you find it boring or repugnant. The law requires (or at least most people assume it does) that children attend school during a certain period of their life. And attendance implies that you be there every day at the given time unless you have a very good reason for not being there—and that reason must be supported by believable adults. An "excuse" from a child in school is not considered trustworthy.

James Herndon suggests that captivity makes everything else about school irrelevant:

> All of the talk about motivation or inspiring kids to learn or innovative courses which are relevant is horseshit. It is horseshit because there is no way to know if students really are interested or not. . . . That is why the school cannot ever learn anything about its students. Why famous psychologists can successfully threaten pigeons into batting ping-pong balls with their wings, but can never learn anything about pigeons.[60]

Dr. Skinner, in his famous experiment, showed that pigeons could be trained to play ping-pong by the use of operant conditioning. Were they really playing ping-pong? Of course, not, they were simply conditioned to perform certain actions, meaningless to the pigeons. In a similar way, school attempts to "motivate" children to do what they're told and follow directions that are meaningless outside the context of school.

In addition to the compartmentalization of time, there are constraints on speech. Children in school may not speak "out of turn" or converse with friends of their choice. They are now expected to heed the directions of a perfect stranger

---

[60] Herndon, *How to Survive in Your Native Land,* 97-98.

called "teacher"—and don't ask questions unless you've been given permission. A young person's endless curiosity will soon be suppressed to conform to the lesson at hand.

One of the stringent messages of school is that you must pay attention to things that don't interest you. Frank Smith believes that not paying attention to what doesn't make sense to you is an important part of learning. "The right to ignore anything that doesn't make sense is a crucial element of any child's learning—and the first right children are likely to lose when they get to the controlled learning environment of school."[61]

The important learning in school is that you have less control over your life than you thought you had; other people are now deciding what's important for you, how you should be spending your time, and even what kind of person you're supposed to be. Your personal interests beyond what's determined by school will be discounted as frivolous. Even in those schools or classrooms where children are given the maximum amount of choice about what they do, those choices are necessarily limited by the school's curriculum and its notions about what activities are appropriate for children of any given age. The individual has no voice and no rights. And the school wants us to believe that this is preparation for participation in a democratic society!

Rewards and Punishments

Once the rules and regulations have been made, they require enforcement. The person or institution that establishes a set of rules for other people must live in fear of looking foolish if those rules are casually disregarded. Therefore,

---

[61] Smith, *Book of Learning and Forgetting*, 19.

sanctions in the form of rewards for being good and punishments for being bad must be exercised.

When brute force doesn't work or is thought to be too harsh, the best way to gain compliance is by persuading your subjects to think that they really want to comply, and that their lack of compliance is a problem of theirs, not of the institution's. Under this method, teachers, when dealing with unruly students, are encouraged to say things like: "It looks like you have a problem. How could I help you solve it?"[62] Even humour may be used to lighten things up: "Said with a smile and an appropriate gesture, this may break the tension and 'allow' the student to sit down because he knows he has made his point."[63] The use of the word "allow" is especially interesting since it suggests that the student is being *allowed* not to do what he or she wants but what the teacher wants. It is the ever-so-subtle way of pushing the notion that children really *do* want to control their behaviour as expected, they just haven't yet learned how.

Clearly, this calls for a set of tactics, which must not be evident to the students. At one time, it was simply a matter of do-what-you're-told-or-suffer-a-caning, but now subtler means are called for. Various contemporary strategies like *Mindfulness* are employed to make it seem as though the students really want to do what they're told, they may just need help in order to do it. Providing help that hasn't been asked for signifies the superiority of the helper and the weakness of the one being helped. The school has abandoned the authoritarian—who-cares-what-you-want?—approach into a form of mind control that says, "*We* know what you really want and we'll help you get it." So control of behaviour becomes a

---

[62] William Glasser, *The Quality School: Managing Students Without Coercion*, (New York: Harper & Row, 1990), 138.
[63] Glasser, *The Quality School*, 139.

problem that the student has; it's a matter of adjustment, of accepting, not so much what you are constrained to do, but what's been defined as good for you. Just as the teacher has to believe that the school is always right, the kids must be convinced or coerced into believing the same.

Shifting the "problem" onto the student is a form of humiliation, implying that your problem is that you don't like being a prisoner and don't like having to perform tasks that bore you and have no relevance to you; you don't know what's good for you or even what you want. Similar methods involve shaming an individual child for not wanting to be part of "our group." Last resorts in dealing with the recalcitrant student may be to enlist the co-operation of the parents or of the school psychologist. If worse comes to worst, there are always drugs like Ritalin to bring the misfits into line.

Of course the good kids will receive appropriate rewards in the same way that the bad kids will be dealt with by psychology or parental intervention. Rewards, or positive reinforcements, are generally considered to be more desirable than punishments and criticisms. Rewarding good behaviour seems so logical and benevolent, all evidence to the contrary notwithstanding.

Harry F. Harlow, the experimental psychologist whose work with rhesus monkeys during the 1940s and 50s is widely known, performed an experiment to see how a food reward would influence monkeys' performance in a puzzle-solving test.[64] The monkeys were first given puzzle devices which involved a series of manipulations leading to the opening of a compartment. In the first part of the experiment, the monkeys were simply given the devices and their actions were

---

[64] Harry F. Harlow & Donald R. Meyer, "Learning motivated by a manipulation drive," Journal of Experimental Psychology, 40, American Psychological Association, 1950, 228-234.

carefully recorded. It was noted that the animals showed considerable curiosity over the puzzles, played with them until they could open the compartment, then repeated the operation numerous times, showing a lively interest in the process of manipulation. In the second part of the experiment, the monkeys were shown that a few raisins were stashed in the compartment and could be retrieved by again solving the puzzle and opening the box. The result was that the monkeys appeared to lose interest in the process of solving the puzzle. They now made many more errors and stopped playing with the devices once the raisins had been removed. Often to the surprise of the researchers, countless other studies have shown that the promise of rewards tends to have an adverse effect upon performance. Numerous studies of this nature are cited in Alfie Kohn's book *Punished by Rewards*.[65] In another book on the subject of the effects of reward-giving, Daniel Pink has this to say about schools: "Unfortunately . . . there's a mismatch between what science knows and what schools do. . . . They're redoubling their emphasis on routines, right answers, and standardization."[66]

In school, the praise and criticism handed out in the form of grades, good or bad, and privileges, granted or withheld, focuses attention on performance—"To offer a prize for doing a deed is tantamount to declaring that the deed is not worth doing for its own sake."[67] —and offers the dubious motivation of knowing that you are either better or worse than your fellow students. Alfie Kohn puts it this way:

---

[65] Alfie Kohn, *Punished by Rewards: The Trouble with Gold Stars, Incentive Plans, A's, Praise, and Other Bribes*, (New York: Houghton Mifflin Company, 1993), 35-48.
[66] Daniel H. Pink, *Drive, the Surprising Truth About What Motivates Us*, (New York: Riverhead Books, 2009), 185.
[67] Neill, *Summerhill,* (New York: Hart Publishing Company Inc., 1960), 162.

The truth is that the problem is not just punishments but also rewards, not bad grades but the emphasis on grading per se. Anything that gets children to think primarily about their performance will undermine their interest in learning, their desire to be challenged, and ultimately the extent of the achievement. Small wonder that rewards have precisely those effects.[68]

A. S. Neill makes a similar statement with his usual forthright vigour:

> Goodness that depends on fear of hell or fear of the policeman or fear of punishment is not goodness at all—it is simply cowardice. Goodness that depends on hope for reward or hope of praise or hope of heaven depends on bribery.[69]

Grades and Tests

Grades and report cards are another way of administering rewards and punishments, approval and disapproval. Because of the way curriculum is structured, it is believed that step by step accomplishments along the way can be measured by carefully designed tests. The school presents the child with a bit of "age appropriate" knowledge or a piece of some skill, drills him or her on it, and then checks up by testing to see whether or not they've "got it." If they haven't got it, then they obviously weren't paying attention or didn't try hard enough. They will either have to be re-taught or given some kind of inferior grade or mark. "You are not as good as the kids who got A's and B's." If a child continues to perform poorly, he or she may be further humiliated by being given "special help" or remedial treatment. If that doesn't work, it

---

[68] Kohn, *Punished by Rewards*, 159.
[69] Neill, *Summerhill*, 129.

may be found—again by testing—that they really are inferior (low IQ), and need to be segregated into special kinds of classes or schools.

The testing upon which school grades are largely based is, at best, a measure of short-term memory. Hence, the tradition of cramming for exams. A person's level of interest in a given matter cannot be measured by a test; too much questioning and thinking will only use up the limited amount of time allowed. Tests are administered under artificial and controlled conditions that have little to do with the real life experiences that add up to learning.

Another problem with tests is that each question has, for the most part, only one right answer. There is no room for being vaguely right. Value is placed on "knowing the answer," while the value of tinkering with things to figure out what works is discounted. Perhaps the real reason for standardized testing is to create anxiety and fear. Isn't that what tests do? Remember the monitors walking up and down the aisles watching out for any evidence of cheating? "Now you'll be sorry you didn't pay attention when you were supposed to!"

Schools have by and large adopted test scores as the measure of their success in doing what they do. Departments of Education point to test results to prove how successfully they have been spending taxpayers' money. In some school districts, test results are even made available to parents so they can see how well their kids are doing and apply pressure if needed. Test scores can even affect the real estate market because parents will choose to purchase houses in school districts that offer the most promising test results for their children. Usually the "good" schools are in the "better" part of town, while the not-so-good schools are where the poor and the immigrants are.

The scramble for high marks in school has led to the creation of a profitable industry for private tutoring institutions which guarantee, for a price, improvement in your child's in-school performance. Parents not only fear that their children may not make it into university when the time comes but also that the public schools are failing to provide a rigorous enough program to ensure the necessary grade point averages. Because the universities have come to rely heavily, even entirely, upon grade point averages, parents are fearful that their youngsters will not make the grade and hence be doomed to lives of indolence and penury.

Fail at School, Fail at Life

Parents who believe that school is the only road to their children's success in later life have reason to be worried. The public schools, in an admirable effort to provide success and avoid failure for all, have eased up on demands of the curriculum. Considering that a good portion of the students in public schools see little reason to be there and have little commitment to their studies, the "dumbing down" of the content of school studies is pretty well a necessity. In their book *The Bell Curve*, Richard Herrnstein and Charles Murray note that:

> The dumbing down of textbooks permeated the textbook market, as publishers and authors strove to satisfy school boards, which routinely applied "readability" formulas to the books they were considering. Thomas Stowell has described a typical example of this process, in which the words *spectacle* and *admired* were deleted from a textbook because they were deemed too difficult for high school students. Stowell compares such timidity to the McGuffey's Readers, the staple text of nineteenth-century children in one-room schoolhouses, pointing out that the

Third Reader used words such as *species, dialogue, heath,* and *benighted*—intended for 8-year-olds.[70]

In recent years, adult illiteracy has been brought to the public attention by various articles and programs. One would expect, or at least hope, that universal schooling would provide for a steady increase in literacy. According to a recent report, this does not seem to be the case:

> There are indications, however, that North American children may be less literate now than they were 55 years ago. In 1945, a U.S. study indicated the average written vocabulary of children aged six to 14 was 25,000 words. A recent study by Cornell University professor Cole Gilbert found the average six- to 14-year-old now has a written vocabulary of 10,000 words. When you consider that in the same period, tens of thousands of words from astronaut to e-mail have been added to the English language, that is troubling news.[71]

Herrnstein and Murray also cite a Wall Street Journal article that quotes an examination from a New Jersey high school in 1885. These are a few of the questions:

> Find the product of $3 \div 4x + 5x2 - 63$ and $4 - 5x - 6x2$.
> Write a sentence containing a noun used as an attribute, a verb in the perfect tense potential mood, and a proper adjective.'
> Name three events of 1777. Which was the most important and why?
> The test was not for high school graduation (which would be impressive enough) but for admission to

---

[70] Richard J. Herrnstein & Charles Murray, *The Bell Curve: Intelligence and Class Structure in American Life*, (New York: The Free Press, 1994), 430-431.
[71] Daphne Bramham, "Illiteracy exacts a grim toll around the world," The Vancouver Sun, Oct. 25, 2000, p. B3.

Jersey City High School. Fifteen-year-olds were supposed to know the answers to these questions.[72]

As the schools have tried to become more humane due to the influence of such people as John Dewey, they have also tried to create a curriculum that would be interesting, even non-threatening, to students. This would have been an admirable goal had the schools and parents been willing to give up the notion of prescribed curriculum altogether and to allow children to follow their own curiosity and interests.

Curriculum

Who decided that learning could be divided up into subjects and that subjects could be divided up into levels and that levels could be divided up into steps that were to be taken one by one in sequence? Why should grade four students, for example, "Ask questions, corroborate inferences, and draw conclusions about the content and origins of different sources." Or that students in grade one are expected to "Identify, organize, and present ideas in a variety of forms." Or that those in grade five should know that "Two equivalent fractions are two ways to represent the same amount (having the same whole)."[73] And what if they don't?

John Gatto concludes, "School's fragmentation of learning into subjects and periods implies that nothing is really important enough to stay with until your curiosity is satisfied."

James Herndon asks:

Who decided that Egypt is just right for seventh graders? Who decided that DNA must be something which all kids

---

[72] Herrnstein & Murray, *The Bell Curve*, 419.
[73] Examples are from "BC's Course Curriculum," (2015), https://curriculum.gov.bc.ca/.

> answer questions about? Who decided that California Indi-
> ans must enter the world of fourth grade kids, or that
> South America must be "learned" by sixth graders?[74]

While he concludes that "Nobody, it seems, made any of these decisions," it's likely that, whoever decided, the system was based upon the inexorable logic of the nineteenth century factory. The factory and the school as we know it were inventions of the Industrial Revolution. Following the "scientific" theories of Frederick Taylor (1865-1915), the work of factories was divided into steps, and each step was performed by one person or group of people. It was not necessary that any given step had to make sense or bear any meaning to the people who were performing it, for according to the plan, the product, a bolt of cloth or a carload of coal, would emerge at the end of the process. Following a similar plan, what do we think the product of school should be?

Another popular model for breaking work into pieces is constructing a building. Buildings are made step by step, starting from the bottom and working up in carefully designed increments. Each step along the way is best completed before the next one begins. You can't put on the siding until the framing is done, and you can't paint the wall until the plaster is dry. This is very much the same as the concept of *scaffolding*, derived from, but not created by, Lev Vygotsky. All very logical and all clearly reducible into steps and stages. The smooth functioning of the factory model school requires all of the features of discipline and curriculum of which we have been speaking, all of the features which are *in direct opposition* to what we know about how learning takes place and how intelligence develops.

The application of these methods to schooling was in contrast to what had been taking place in the unorganized

---

[74] Herndon, *How to Survive in Your Native Land*, 101-102.

one-room school, in which older children were frequently called upon to teach younger ones, and all levels of age, ability, and accomplishment were thrown together. Attendance was sporadic and grade-level was determined by accomplishment rather than age. In that kind of school, and prior to legislated compulsory attendance, failure was virtually unknown.[75]

As governments took more control of schools and required uniformity and predictability, children were segregated by age, seated in tidy rows, and expected to perform the same tasks at the same time with little or no individual interaction with one another. Though the modern school still segregates by grade or division, it has for the most part done away with rows of desks bolted to the floor though not entirely with silent lines of children marching from class to class. Contrary

---

[75] Richard Fidler, "One Room Schools A Hundred Years Ago: Of Study Time, Recitations, and Recess," Grand Traverse Journal, July 9, 2018, https://gtjournal.tadl.org/2018/one-room-schools-a-hundred-years-ago-of-study-time-recitations-and-recess/.

to modern trends, proponents of the so-called "traditional" schools, longed for by many parents, see a return to an older style of school and of teaching as a way to re-establish the values they would like to see upheld by a market-based society. These schools are supposed to emphasize drill, conformity, and obedience.

But many elements of the factory school are prevalent in even the most progressive of public schools. Punctuality is a required virtue, children are segregated into grades, the day is divided into periods, the teacher still calls the shots, and the curriculum is divided into incremental steps. All of this says that learning shall take place according to a pre-set plan devised by experts, success will be rewarded and non-conformity will be punished. Success in school is predicated upon a student's willingness to conform to that plan. In fact, conforming is not enough, it is necessary to *believe* that the school's plan is the only one that can assure success in later life—and woe to the disbeliever.

The Catholic Church decrees that there is no salvation outside the Church. Public school proclaims that there is no education outside of school. As John Holt put it: "But now all roads lead through school. To fail there is to fail everywhere. What they write about you there, often in secret, follows you for life. There is no escape from it and virtually no appeal."[76] Fail at school, fail at life.

Conclusion

While these comments may seem unduly harsh or cynical, the important point is that school controls, and it controls by

---

[76] John Holt, *What Do I Do Monday?* (New York: E. P. Dutton & Co., Inc., 1970), 57.

threat, shame, and humiliation, no matter how pleasantly these may be delivered. School assaults the child's self-esteem by saying, in effect, "We know what's good for you—you don't." And it will elicit obedience to its dictates by whatever means are currently fashionable. The fact that there are many teachers who do their best to make school interesting and pleasant for their pupils does not alter the fact that once in school, you have given up control of your own life—even to the extent of being able to discover on your own what kind of person you are.

The school will make every effort to intrude upon your personal life by assigning homework. New technologies are making it increasingly difficult for children to escape the control of the school. No longer will the excuse "a dog ate it" even be worth considering when computer programs like *Class Dojo*[77] can track a student's every assignment and every move, communicate secretly with parents, and insinuate the influence of school into home and private life. Now that most student work, in or out of school, is done on a computer or computer tablet, and on line, the teacher can monitor the kid's work at any time.

Whether you comply and do as you're told or rebel and raise hell, you are doing it because of school and for the school's ultimate benefit or detriment, not yours.

The Swiss psychiatrist Alice Miller has written about what she calls "poisonous pedagogy" or any method, program, school, or system which imposes one person's will upon another. Anytime we do this, any time we try to "help" someone who has not asked for help, anytime we think we know what's good for another person, we are inviting participation in a battle, however subtle, for power, individuality—and control. She has summed it up thus:

---

[77] https://www.google.com/search?client=firefox-b-d&q=Class+Dojo

You know, now I wonder if what is called pedagogy may not be simply a question of power, and if we shouldn't be speaking and writing much more about hidden power struggles instead of racking our brains about finding better methods of child-rearing.[78]

---

[78] Alice Miller, *For Your Own Good: Hidden Cruelty in Child-rearing and the Roots of Violence*, H. & H. Hannum, trans, (New York: Farrar, Straus, Giroux, 1983), 277. Original work published in 1980.

MAKING SCHOOLS
THAT ARE GOOD FOR KIDS

Every child is an individual marvel, gifted with unique capacities, ready to respond to those who trust them and to those who have no fear of giving them freedom.—Lady Allen[79]

All children should be tirelessly noisy, playful, grubby-handed except at meal times, soiling and tearing such clothes as they need wear, bringing not only the joy of childhood into the house but dust and mud as well.[80]—George Bernard Shaw.

It will be evident to the reader by now that this writer has nothing positive to say about schools as they presently exist. Of course, it's easy to criticize, especially an institution that is already under attack from many sources, but the question will inevitably be asked, "All right then, what do you propose to replace it with?" Let's say that school should simply be abolished. After all, the world doesn't fall apart during the summer when most kids are not in school. However, given the structure of contemporary society in which many parents are working away from home, and the streets of our cities and the commerce that is carried in them are not congenial to the presence of young people, it appears unavoidable to provide an institution which can offer protection, care, and growth-enhancing experience to our young.

---

[79] Allen and Nicholson, *Memoirs of an Uneducated Lady*, 43.
[80] George Bernard Shaw, *The London Times*, August 2, 1944, cited in Allen *Memoirs*.

Rights and Freedoms

The question now is how do we create a school, or something like a school, that offers free access to whatever kids may need or want to learn and to grant to them all the rights that are due to any person living in a democratic society.

Let's look at what is guaranteed by the Canadian Charter of Rights and Freedoms. The Charter specifies that *everyone* has

1) Freedom of conscience and religion;
2) Freedom of thought, belief, opinion and expression;
3) Freedom of peaceful assembly, and
4) Freedom of association.

Note that *everyone* is not limited by age, ability, or anything else. It is simply everyone. Doesn't this powerfully suggest that children have these rights just as much as anyone else. I've already noted how children are deprived of their basic rights when they are in school. In our school children and adults (*everyone*) are free to associate with whomever they choose and to assemble in groups of whatever composition they wish. We also assure freedom of thought, belief, opinion, and expression. This means that everyone is free to develop thoughts and ideas of their own and to express them in whatever way they choose. Again keeping in mind the basic concept: You are free to do whatever you like as long as you don't interfere with anyone else's freedom. You can see right away that our kids will have almost unlimited freedom, while necessarily including respect for the freedom of others.

Under *Legal Rights*, "everyone has the right to life, liberty and security of the person and the right not to be deprived thereof except in accordance with the principles of fundamental justice." Let's remember that the right not to be deprived of liberty and security of person again applies to *every-*

102

one. Continuing, we are informed that "Everyone has the right not to be arbitrarily detained or imprisoned." (What was that school story I heard about detentions?)

We've all heard about "any cruel and unusual treatment or punishment" that everyone has the right *not* to be subjected to. I'm sure your principal will tell you that nothing "cruel or unusual" ever happens in school. All I can say is: that's debatable.[81]

The citizen's right to vote, as stated in the Charter, in federal or provincial elections is now limited to those age 18 or over, though there is considerable discussion about lowering that age to 16. Doesn't that suggest that we'd better give our kids some experience in democratic processes before we send them to the voting booth? Community meetings in our school will provide just that. This will be explained in detail later.

I want to talk a bit about "security of person" especially where children are concerned. Wouldn't "security" in this case suggest physical and mental well-being? That's why our school will provide full dental and health care as well as a guarantee of freedom from any kind of mental oppression, like the imposition of certain beliefs.

I suggest that our society has traditionally deprived children of freedom of conduct and expression because of the erroneous notion that children have to be disciplined, managed, and controlled according to some Calvinistic moral teachings supported by the behaviourist views of John Locke, J. B. Watson, Frederick Taylor, B. F. Skinner, and all the others. In direct contradiction, our school believes that the instinct to grow and to learn will flourish in an atmosphere of

---

[81] As an amusing if not frightening example see: "15 Types of Punishments Used in Schools in 2023" https://thinkstudent.co.uk/types-of-punishment-used-in-schools/. Yes, there are people who believe that children, like criminals, must be punished.

freedom and approval. We will provide a supportive and lov-ing atmosphere based on the understanding that love is "un-conditional positive regard." This necessarily includes a belief in the basic goodness of human nature.

How will our children learn? The real answer to this ques-tion is: You can't stop them. I believe that children are natu-rally driven to explore their environment and learn what they need to know following their own direction and curiosity. Remember that children (and scientists) learn through a pro-cess of trial and error. The more time and space we allow for this kind of playful approach to learning and discovery, the greater the benefits to all involved.

Because learning is as natural and necessary as growth, we want to provide nourishment for body *and* mind. That's why kids at our school will be well fed. The security that comes from knowing that food, warmth, and human contact will never be withheld is a requirement. No one can learn and grow into being healthy in all respects without it.

Children will grow into the culture in which they find themselves. Therefore, our school will also be populated by adults who are living rich and fulfilling lives and are happy to share their time and interests with children and young people. This means that people of all ages will be creating and doing things together. Life can become an exciting adventure. It's really very simple: You learn from the company you keep.

The school I am proposing would not look like the schools of today. It might resemble a small village or even a one-room school set in a playground. It could be possible to create small neighbourhood schools of the one-room type or larger urban schools of the village type. In either case, the school would be open to youngsters of, say, five years of age on up to young people of high school age or beyond, prepar-ing to enter university or work. Any youngster would be free to drop out after the age of, say, fourteen. In such a school there would be no segregation of ages, no curriculum, no compulsory classes, no grades, no textbooks, no testing of any kind, and no scoring or marking. Yes, structured lessons in traditional school subjects would be available to anyone of any age that wanted them. Preparation for state exams or university entrance would be available. This school recognizes that there is more than one way to learn. As A. S. Neill and many others have pointed out, the method of teaching is irrelevant if the desire to learn is there.

The school would provide a large variety of opportunities for play and discovery. There would be an active association with the surrounding community with programs similar to apprenticeships and mentorships. Association with knowledgeable and experienced adults would be key, and such associations can happen in or out of the school. These are people who are open and able to share their knowledge and experience. There will be reading and talking, cooking and eating, work and play, teaching and learning. Adults, young children, and teenagers can freely join together in all kinds of projects and activities.

Again, classes or lessons would be offered without any expectation of participation. Our children will seek out "more knowledgeable others"[82] in pursuit of their own curiosity or interest. The results would be unpredictable, just as life itself is unpredictable and full of opportunities for learning and enlightenment. Above all, the school and the people in it believe that children are ready and able to take on their own education. The school does not give guidance and direction unless asked for, it gives freedom.

In a school that is truly democratic there would be regular meetings in which every person—child or adult—has a free voice and one vote in any and all decisions affecting life at the

As seen in the Zone of Proximal Development.

school. Every person from five-years-old and up has an equal opportunity to form and express their thoughts and opinions.[83]

We know that a truly democratic society provides for the security and needs of its citizens, so our school would provide full medical and dental care, at least two full meals every day, clothing when necessary, and protection of person when needed. Each individual, regardless of age, in the school is entitled to equal and non-judgmental treatment.

The Concept

My concept of the school that is good for kids is based on three institutions and one book.

The adventure playground (*Abenteuerspielplatz*)

The Book of Learning and Forgetting (Frank Smith)

The Saturna Island Free School

Prescott College (Prescott, Arizona)

Each is based on the principle that people—yes, that includes children—learn and grow best in an atmosphere of approval, freedom, and individual responsibility.

---

[83] For a good example of how this works, see *Summerhill (2008)*: https://rb.gy/xknaun. "Best freedom movie ever!"

The Adventure Playground

Every school should be an adventure playground.

Abenteuerspielplarz Eller, Düsseldorf, Germany

I once had the pleasure and delight of accompanying two of my grandchildren to the *Abenteuerspielplatz* in Düsseldorf, Germany. What I saw was a wondrous conglomeration of pathways, tunnels, waterways, ponds and puddles, curious structures, large pipes, tires, rope swings, trees, bushes, and plants. There was one area piled up with boards and bits of lumber, saws, hammers, nails, all manner of building materials and tools with which kids could build huts and forts to their hearts' content. Not far from there was a campfire around which kids were toasting marshmallows and roasting wieners. A kiosk dispensing juices and water was nearby. Suppose you felt like throwing things, within easy reach was an open area abutting a tall berm. Several boys were enthusiastically throwing rocks, of which there was a plentiful supply, at painted

107

and imaginary targets on the berm. Children of all ages were dashing about, playing quietly in a leafy corner, paddling in a pond, or riding around the dirt track. It was chaotic and wonderful!

The glory of the *Spielplatz* is that it is largely unsupervised. Not entirely, however. If *supervised* is the right term, there were, mixed in with the kids, a number of adults or high school age young people joining in the play or offering a helping hand here or there, while not directing activities in any way. At the campfire, for example, a man was enjoying the scene while keeping an eye out for the very rare incident requiring attention. There might be people there cooking, painting, making pottery or other activities that kids are free to participate in—or not. Many such playgrounds offer a variety of craft and art material, readily available. Other adventure playgrounds also have animals that kids can play with, pet, and enjoy. The atmosphere is one of freedom and the joy of being young, free, and alive.

Giving kids a chance to play freely and without adult-designed equipment and games occurred to a Danish landscape architect, Carl Theodor Sørenson who noticed that children enjoyed playing in abandoned construction sites and junkyards rather than his beautifully designed parks and playgrounds. Seeing children playing with sticks, stones, boxes, ropes, water, sand, mud, old tires, whatever might be lying around, he envisioned "A junk playground in which children could create and shape, dream and imagine a reality."[84] He created the first "junk playground" (*skrammellegepladser*) in 1943 in Emdrup, Denmark. Lady Allen (You should know her by now.) later wrote:

---

[84] Quoted in "Adventure Playgrounds, a children's world in the city," http://adventureplaygrounds.hampshire.edu/history.html, accessed June 17, 2023.

> I was completely swept off my feet by my first visit to Emdrup playground. In a flash of understanding I realized that I was looking at something quite new and full of possibilities. There was a wealth of waste material on it and no man-made fixtures. The children could dig, build houses, experiment with sand, water or fire and play games of adventure and make believe.[85]

This led her to campaign for what she renamed "adventure playgrounds" to be created on the World War II bombsites in the United Kingdom.

If you're a worrying parent or teacher, you must be thinking that this would be asking for trouble. Won't the kids just go wild, get hurt, wreck things, fight, or just waste their time? This is another example of how common assumptions about children lead us astray, because when given freedom to play freely and without supervision kids are remarkably careful and observing of the needs of others. This is especially true when all ages are free to associate. Younger children will have a chance to identify with and learn from older kids, and the older kids will learn about nurturing and care for the young. Basic human opportunities that are denied any young person in a standard school.

Liberty

As defined by John Stuart Mill in his book *On Liberty,*[86] the guiding principle is that you may do whatever you like as

---

[85] Cited in *Play and Playground Encyclopedia: Lady Allen Hurtwood,* https://www.pgpedia.com/l/lady-allen-hurtwood, accessed June 17, 2023.

[86] John Stuart Mill, 1806-1873. *On Liberty* was first published in 1859.

long as you do not infringe on anyone else's freedom. This is what A. S. Neill called *Freedom not Licence*. This is laid out in a statement from the Summerhill School website:

> Summerhill's aim is to allow children to grow naturally, to experience personal freedom, to play and develop at their own pace and to go in their own direction whilst taking responsibility for their own actions and the community around them. We believe in freedom but not licence. This means that you are free to do as you like—but you must not interfere with somebody else's freedom. You are free to go to lessons, or stay away, because that is your own personal business, but you cannot play your drum kit at four in the morning because it would keep other people awake.[87]

And the result? As a government report on Summerhill School observed, "Behaviour is good. Pupils are polite, well-mannered and courteous. Bullying is rare. As a result, pupils feel safe at school."[88] Quite a contrast to the twenty-first century school where it is now considered advisable to have a police officer present at all times.

It is true that kids who have been ruled over, threatened, and judged, will break loose given the chance. Any free-schooler will recognize this as the "wild period" that usually lasts only a few weeks. It says, "Yay, I'm free, I can do whatever I want!" It doesn't take long for the wild period to close and the former trouble-makers to find that being a responsible member of a free community is way more rewarding. He or she will soon find out as well that the democratic community meeting offers a voice and support and participation in

[87] A. S. Neill Summerhill School, https://www.summerhillschool.co.uk/freedom-not-licence.
[88] Office for Standards in Education (Ofsted), "School Report, Summerhill School," accessed Jan. 31, 2021, https://files.ofsted.gov.uk/v1/file/50075777/.

decision making. The former "problem" is now a free and equal member of a democratic society.

The Book of Learning and Forgetting

If you've read this or anything else I've written, you'll know that I am a great fan of Frank Smith (1928-2020), especially of the book in the title above. Smith was what is known as a cognitive psychologist or psycholinguist, only fancy ways of saying that he studied how and why people think. This is what led him to pursue the study of reading. His first academic book *Understanding Reading*[89], published in 1971 and now running to six editions, created a sensation among teachers and educators who had long puzzled over methods of teaching kids to read. Nothing seemed to work, and even Rudolf Flesch's also sensational book *Why Johnny Can't Read—And What You Can Do About It*[90] with its endless drills in phonics (mad, sad, glad, fad, cad) didn't seem to improve the ability to read—or increase interest in reading. In sharp contrast, Smith recommended a whole language approach or simply starting with understanding and thinking. As he famously wrote, "You learn to read by reading."[91] Everyone will learn to read when they see a need to read. There is no reason why every six-year-old should be subjected to reading instruction.

This is not about various methods of instruction, but a reflection on how reading and writing fit into our ideas of the school that is good for kids. We know that kids who come

---

[89] Frank Smith, *Understanding Reading, A Psycholinguistic Analysis of Reading and Leaning to Read* (New York: Holt, Rinehart and Winston, 1971).
[90] Rudolf Flesch, *Why Johnny Can't Read—And What You Can Do About It* (New York: Harper and Brothers, 1955).
[91] Smith, *Book of Learning and Forgetting*, 29.

from homes where reading is a common activity and where people read to each other will almost always know how to read and how to enjoy reading. Even a baby cuddled on mom's or dad's lap as they page through a book and read will be associating the spoken word with the printed word. At the school that is good for kids reading is a major activity. Adults and older kids read aloud to younger kids or anyone who wants to listen. This can happen spontaneously or at chosen times of the day or evening. Again, there are no requirements, but I think it's safe to assume that most people, especially small children, love being read to. Every school will have a library or access to a library where there is unlimited free choice of books to read or look at. Banning of books will be unheard of because we trust intelligence to weed out the bad from the good. When reading is seen as enjoyable and not accompanied by any kind of lessons or drills, it becomes a pleasurable and communal activity.

This brings us to the second major concept from Frank Smith's writing that will be essential to the good school: "We learn from the company we keep, throughout our lives, without effort, without awareness, and with no forgetting."[92] I'm sure you can see how this is contrary to the school idea of teaching, memorizing, and testing—methods that require effort, application, and, as far as testing goes, forgetting. So, our school will not have teaching unless it's asked for and will never have any kind of tests or grades of its own. While any student who wants to can study, with or without instruction, if preparing to write some government or university examination, our children will always be learning from the others they can spend time with.

If we accept that *we learn from the company we keep* our school will provide complete freedom of association. That is,

---

[92] Smith, *Book of Learning and Forgetting*, 30.

children are free to hang around or play with whomever they wish, regardless of age or accomplishment. This means that the school—let's call it the community—has a number of adults of many different interests and abilities who are there to associate with kids, in work and in play. Imagine, for example, a resident writer and illustrator of children's books, a musical ensemble like a string quartet, several carpenters who are building a house, a technology expert who is repairing computers, or a mathematician who is working on various projects. The possibilities are as endless as the curiosity that drives learning and intelligence.

What would this look like? The best comparison I can think of is that it's like a large child-loving and freedom-loving family, perhaps not unlike one in a hunting and gathering community. Everyone goes about their own business and joins up with groups or individuals as they please. Little kids will play and play and play. Bigger kids will play organized games, build forts, play music, and learn skills like cooking or woodworking; they will read books and engage in bull sessions. At all times there are grownups either taking part in kids' play, reading to kids, or engaged in their own serious work. The grownups in this big family are people who know how to do things, are busy doing them, and are always willing to share with anyone who is interested. They are not there as "teachers," they are not trained in any special teaching methods nor do they have a bag of tricks to "motivate" students. Since we ascribe to the motto *we learn from the company we keep*, we'll want to have people around who are doing interesting and worthwhile things. Vygotsky's Zone of Proximal Development suggests that we learn best from a "knowledgeable other," and it is the community's responsibility to provide knowledgeable others for our kids to hang out with.

Here is something that I learned in school at about age nine. Faced with impossible (for me) tasks of addition and long division, I learned that when it came to arithmetic and anything to do with numbers, I was not a person to whom such matters would ever be comprehensible. I decided that I was simply not very smart. How often do we teach kids that they are stupid and incompetent by forcing them to do things they don't understand or have no interest in? A point that Frank Smith makes again and again is that we are learning all the time and that learning takes place effortlessly and without forgetting. The catch is that we are probably not learning what school teachers or other authority figures think we are learning. Just as I learned that I was "not very smart" instead of the addition and long division I was being taught.

Suppose, on the other hand, I had met a mathematician (as I did in later life) whose enthusiasm for computation and numerical wonders was contagious, I might have developed an interest in mathematics. I might have gone on to study and learn more about this fascinating field. I didn't pursue those studies because I had other interests, but I did learn to respect the importance and value of accomplishment in mathematics. I still think it would be fun to learn more about equations, cosines, calculus, prime numbers, and even the Fibonacci sequence. This reminds me of something that the conductor Benjamin Zander said in a TED talk: "Everybody loves classical music—they just haven't found out about it yet." [93] Wouldn't this apply to just about everything? It all depends upon how and from whom we learn.

---

[93] Benjamin Zander, "The transformative power of classical music," TED2008, YouTube video, 20:22, https://www.ted.com/talks/benjamin_zander_the_transformative_power _of_classical_music?language=en.

Joining a Club

Frank Smith presents us with this charming vignette: "Relatives and friends surround the baby and say in effect, 'Welcome, stranger. You're one of us.' And the baby looks up and responds, 'Hi, folks, I must be just like you.'"[94] This is, also in effect, joining the club of the people you know and feel to be part of. This will involve learning the multitude of societal exactitudes, from knowing about what kind of eye contact is acceptable to learning to speak the same way as the people around you speak.

Joining the club simply means that you are taking on some characteristics of the people you identify with—as you see them. As we grow up, we encounter many more people: members of the family, grandparents, uncles and aunts, friends, teachers, authors in the books we read, countless associations of one kind or another that we form with others. All offering us clubs to join. Of course you will not necessarily take on *all* the characteristics of the club, nor will you always join a club that is good for you. The important thing to remember is, and I'll say it again: we learn from the company we keep. I can't emphasize enough that it is the job of the school to offer constructive and interesting people to associate with—interesting and constructive clubs to join.

One final comment on this subject: the key concept is *identify with*. That doesn't necessarily mean the people that are thought to be good for you or that you are mostly exposed to. Smith asks us who do kids in school hear talking the most and who do they talk like. Yes, they hear teachers and others in authority talking all the time, but they don't talk like those

---

[94] Smith, *Book of Learning and Forgetting*, 17.

people, they talk like their friends, the people they identify with, and the clubs they belong to.

During pandemic school closures, I heard some kids being interviewed about what they missed about school. Do you think it was the lessons or the teachers? No. In every case it was "my friends." Does this mean that trying to offer associations beyond age groups is hopeless? Clearly I'm saying *no* because children, as well as anyone, will gravitate toward interesting, non-judgmental, and active adults and older kids. These people are not authorities that can impose judgment on your behaviour or learning, they are just active and interesting open-minded individuals. I'm talking about the kind of education that, say, Mozart would have had or that, in even earlier times, Socrates would have provided. The aim is to re-establish a positive relationship between adults and children. Consequently, adults associated with the school would necessarily be non-judgmental, intelligent, learned, and thoughtful. They would also love being with children without attempting to improve or correct them. They would be people who retained a childlike ability to perceive the world with wonder and delight. They would be people who could engage in play with children without condescension or ulterior motives.

116

The Saturna Island Free School

Saturna Island Free School

Imagine a twenty-eight acre rural property with trees, wilderness, pastures, barns, a private beach, an orchard, a big beautiful 1890s house, and a large forested area directly adjoining, all located on one of British Columbia's gulf islands. This is but an inadequate description of the Saturna Island Free School. Could there possibly have been a more perfect place for kids to play, to explore, or to hang out together in the big kitchen or the panelled dining room or to read quietly in the well-stocked library? This is where it all happened starting in the fall of 1968.

I remember sitting around the dining table of my house in Burnaby creating a brochure and announcement of the opening. We were offering a boarding school for kids of all ages. I think then we set a price of $1000 for a school year. Looking

117

back, it seems like we were running head on into unknown territory. Well, not entirely, because I, as the only certified teacher, had had experience both with my class of unique youngsters in Williams Lake[95] and with a tumultuous half year at The New School in Vancouver. Remember that the 1960s were years of "Yes, we can do this!" Anything seemed possible.

It didn't take long for the registrations to start coming in. By the time we opened in September, there were about thirty kids ready to move in. We had a bunch of teenagers, a couple of little kids, and a few ten-to-twelve-year olds. There were six of us, Bill, Cathy, Gretel, Rini, Lyn, and me. We were often joined from time to time by other people we knew as well as a few faithful New School parents. A ratio of this many adults to thirty kids had any regular school beat hands down.

How did it all come to this? Well, when I was teaching in a public elementary school in a small city in British Columbia, I wrote an article or two about my thoughts on the workings of school—critical of course. Since I had been reading Carl Rogers and A. S. Neill, I was taken by the idea of non-direction and freedom. Some people from an "alternative" school in Vancouver read what I wrote and offered me the job of headmaster. *The New School*, as it was called, was started by a few university professors who thought a Summerhill-type school would be good for their kids.

Since I knew for sure that I could not survive much longer in the oppressive public school atmosphere, I eagerly accepted the job. The line I spoke to those who were hiring me was indeed about freedom for kids based on the *Summerhill* model. Alas, some of the parents were horrified when their kids showed no interest in lessons but preferred to dash

---

[95] This is covered in detail in my other book *School and the End of Intelligence.*

about madly, yelling obscenities, or flooding the basement. There were, however, a number of parents who thought it was all great, and they saw that the kids were loving it. Two factions developed, and after many intense and excruciating meetings, the school split apart, half the parents supporting me and half, the half that owned the school building, wanting to revert to some kind of structured school-like program.

Without any place to land, we had a flock of freedom-

A free school student

loving kids arriving at our house in Burnaby every morning. They ran around, climbed in and out of windows and conducted themselves in ways unacceptable to a middle-class neighbourhood. All we could do was to pile them all into a Volkswagen van that we had been given and invade various parks and public spaces in the city. All this time, we were looking for some place where we could set up a school. At first we focused on city properties, without luck, until a listing for a property on an island proved irresistible. We went to see it and the Saturna Island Free School was born.

I can only add that we were idealistic, fearless, and naïve risk-takers. After we moved in, there was an enormous amount of work to do before the kids started to arrive, but we were undaunted because we were in pursuit of an ideal. And it was an ideal that we all believed in.

So what happened? First of all, let me remind the reader that this was more than fifty years ago, and while it lives

119

brightly in my memory, I'm sure that memory has levelled up what had to have been many difficulties. Anyway, getting on with the story, it all went very well. The older kids would gather in one of the cabins, stay up all night, indulge in whatever (we didn't know or care), come into the house to listen to the latest Beatles and Led Zeppelin records or to engage in all-night bull sessions mostly with Bill, who was much liked by the older kids. All the younger kids played and played, as well they should because they had all these most inviting places to explore. This isn't to say that older and younger kids kept separate, not at all. They often played together or little kids would sit around listening to grownup talk. Meal times and evenings were great gathering times, everyone seated around the big dining table, talking this and that, laughing, and becoming, as it soon became clear, a community like one big happy family. Were there problems? Of course there were: a few broken windows, skinned knees, and rare disagreements. I do not remember a single incident of bullying.

Did anyone do any school work? No. Everyone was far too busy to think of having classes or lessons.

We did occasionally teach or tutor someone who asked for something specific. One girl, for example, wanted to study Latin, and a boy who lived on the island came daily for tutoring in Grade Ten curriculum. The girl and I worked on Latin grammar until her curiosity was satisfied, and the boy took the Provincial exams and passed. Oh yes, we had an illustrated school newsletter, the *Freeschool Freakout*, with my son Miles as editor. He later became a journalist and professional editor. At the same time, many of us were reading and talking about books. I was listening to opera and classical music in the library, often joined by one or two kids. Unlike Summerhill, the model on which this was all based, we never succeeded in having regular community meetings, one vote per person. As it turned out, we just didn't need to. Things got hashed out around the kitchen table or in ad hoc groups here and there. It was smooth-running anarchy.

It went on for three glorious years, though increasingly plagued by authorities who couldn't abide the idea of children

How "classes" were held at the Free School
Saturna Island photos by David Manning

not being kept under rigid control. Yes, the place was often messy and seemingly disorganized, rather like life itself. What these kids were learning, well, what all of us were learning, was how to live as part of a community, how to take control of your own life, how to learn, and how to live joyously and with purpose.

Freedom

The Saturna Island Free School and all of the schools that subscribed to the idea of Summerhill, believed that children have the right to direct and regulate their own lives in an atmosphere of freedom and support. We need to let children know that we are on their side, that we approve of them as they are, and that they are not expected to live up to any arbitrary rules, regulations, or curricula. Freedom itself becomes regulating. When children are free to play together, they will figure out their own rules of the game. Free kids are not interested in dominating or controlling others; that happens on the public school playground when the anger built up from hours of confinement explodes. Suppression leads to hate; freedom leads to love.

Freedom also leads to health, both physical and mental. When kids are free to play, run around, climb trees, and splash in mud and water, they breathe freely, sleep soundly, and eat well. Their eyes sparkle with interest and curiosity. They are eager to learn about everything. When children are free to learn, they learn quickly and easily. I'm changing the Latin saying *mens sana in corpore sano* to *mens libera in corpore libero*. A free mind in a free body.

Prescott College

Prescott College is a private college in Arizona that advertised itself as being "For the liberal arts and the environment." Since I attended there some twenty-four years ago, the mission has evolved somewhat, becoming more inclusive and more explanatory. The current website states the mission of the college: "To create problem solvers who lead the way to a just and sustainable world."[96] To elaborate, we read: "We believe that classrooms extend beyond four walls" and "We encourage a culture of creativity, collaborative critical thinking, and innovation by teaching courses that challenge established norms and paradigms."

A "class" at Prescott College
permission requested

I can best explain why I believe that this school is offering what I consider the best form of higher education by de-

---

[96] https://prescott.edu/

123

scribing my own experience there. It was in 1999 that I decided to seek a Master's Degree in some form of counselling psychology. It did happen that I had a bit of money from the recent sale of my house on Hornby Island, so I started searching for an ideal in distance learning. I was highly motivated and did not want to sit in classrooms or follow a set curriculum. I had already taken some training in Transactional Analysis,[97] and I thought it would lend credibility to my counselling practice if I had MA after my name. And, besides, I was excited by the idea of being free to study and learn more. I was favourably impressed by what I read about Prescott College, so I enrolled.

First off, one chooses a major, mine was Counselling Psychology. I was assigned a faculty advisor who was to plan my studies with me. There were certain course requirements, but how they were to be fulfilled was to be determined by me and my advisor. She and I discussed what books I would study and what I would hope to accomplish. Also required was attendance at colloquia at the college, once every semester. But that wasn't all, there was a detailed study plan, for the three terms, to be worked out as well as ten study packets to be submitted throughout the full calendar year. Then there was a "qualifying paper" of considerable substance to be written toward the last term and a full master's thesis for graduation. This was not a "cake course," there was a lot of work—self-directed work. Studies had to spring from curiosity and interest, not from a desire for grades or a need to pass tests. This was self-motivated and self-designed learning. To my way of thinking this is how all learning should be pursued. Yes, even in kindergarten, elementary school, and high school; the learner is in charge. Help is available if wanted,

---

[97] You can find details on the International Transactional Analysis Association website: https://www.itaaworld.org/).

but there is no pre-set program or method. And certainly no tests or exams!

At Prescott College, instead of grades of any kind, written self-evaluations, with comments by the advisor, are attached to each course. The student is in charge of evaluating his or her own learning and studies..

All of this was just right for me, and I worked and studied and wrote voluminously over the year. I thoroughly enjoyed the visits to the college in Arizona, especially meeting with the other students. (I was considerably older than any of them.) As required, I gave two lecture-type presentations, one called Paradigms of the Classroom[98] and the other was an Introduction to Transactional Analysis. My qualifying paper was on ADHD and my thesis, on which this book is based, ran to over one hundred pages and created quite a stir. What was so special about this experience was the independence it offered to any motivated student. The students are expected to pursue their studies out of personal interest, curiosity, and motivation, the demands are high, and the support and collaborative nature contribute to the excitement of studying, writing, and learning. This was not a quick and easy way to get a degree; it meant self-motivation and dedication to what I like to think of as the disinterested pursuit of knowledge, in other words, what schools and colleges should be all about.

I like to refer to *the disinterested pursuit of knowledge* as the ideal of study and scholarship. *Disinterested* does not mean uninterested. One source defines it as "not influenced by consideration of personal advantage." In other words, it is the pursuit of knowledge for its own sake, not for pleasing some authority or aiming for a grade or passing a test.[99]

---

[98] There is a chapter with this title in *School and the End of Intelligence."*
[99] "I think an academic is concerned, in a somewhat exclusive way, with getting at deep intellectual truth and maintaining total intellectual

Lessons, Courses, and Studies

Why couldn't these ideas apply to any level of learning or study? Remember that at Summerhill no one is required to attend classes or take any kind of lessons, but many kids decide to do so either because of interest or a desire to reach a personal goal, similar to my plan to acquire an MA, mainly because I simply wanted to. Our school would offer courses leading to high school graduation or other certification, open to anyone and strictly by choice. Wouldn't it be interesting to see kids of varying ages learning together, for example, about physics? No reason why a teenager could not study together with an eight-year-old. In fact, they would have a great deal to offer each other. This is true of any course of studies or engagement in interesting activities. Age is not, or should not be, an issue. In short, unlike public schools, our school will not separate children or adults by age. In a co-operative society all ages work and play together.

What we are proposing is a school that would radically alter our society. We are suggesting that the end result of a practical and benevolent school would be a society that valued intellectual and artistic achievement above status, a society that accepted stewardship of the environment, a society that would give more than lip service to concepts of equality, democracy, and equal opportunity.

---

consistency without letting other considerations interfere." Ed Broadbent, *Seeking Social Democracy, Seven Decades in the Fight for Equality* (Toronto: ECW Press, 2023), 27.

Education and Democracy

How can we create a democratic society if we continue to subject our kids to twelve or more years of the dictatorial authority of school in which they have no say about the operations of the institution or what it requires them to do? They cannot participate in decisions about their own education any more than they can decide how to spend their days or with whom to associate. How can we expect our young people then to become co-operative individuals taking part in democratic decision making?

How can a child develop their listening and reasoning skills if they cannot participate in decision making? I mean making decisions that result from group deliberation in which each person has an equal voice and an equal vote. The outcome will then be determined by a simple majority rather than an authoritarian command. This is a big change from the way schools are run and the way children are treated, but it is a change that recognizes the value of each person regardless of age or status in a true democracy. This is the foundation of education in a free society.

Life in a democratic society implies involvement in the institutions, politics, and government of that society. But that's not what's happening. Participation in civic discourse in the United States has declined in inverse proportion to levels of schooling.[100] Sadly, Canada is following suit. It is also well known that the United States has the lowest level of voter turnout of any of the democratic nations of the world. It would seem that an education system would vigorously direct itself toward changing this situation. However, this has not

---

[100] Robert D. Putnam, *Bowling Alone*, (Journal of Democracy, John Hopkins University Press, 6:1), 65-78.

been the case. An active citizen in a democracy, therefore, would participate in civic discourse, be politically aware, and have a strong belief that his or her voice could make a difference to society and to government. The school that's good for kids is where this starts.

But of course, that's only part of it. The very notion of education might suggest that people would be acquainted with their own culture and history, have a lively interest in other cultures, a sense of responsibility toward the earth and its environment, and are living lives that are rich in emotional and intellectual experience, imagination, and creativity. Sounds good, doesn't it? But we know that these are attributes that are passed on by association with knowledgeable others, not by structured lesson plans and teaching to a captive audience.

The reader will by now have noticed that I have not talked much about bodies of knowledge or skills in any of the traditional academic fields, nor to the holding of degrees or of status, professional or otherwise. Our main concern is to propose a public institution that *enables* young people to develop, learn, and grow in their own way and to facilitate the pursuit of their own interests and passions. Like intelligence, as observed earlier, education is not quantifiable. As Alfie Kohn says, "The job of educators is neither to make students motivated nor to sit passively; it is to set up the conditions that make learning possible."[101]

Writing at an earlier time, Caroline Pratt observed:

> Life in school is only another setting for life anywhere. If we were preparing our children to live under an autocratic

---

[101] Kohn, *Punished by Rewards,* 199.

regime I could understand the need for iron discipline, for suppression of playfulness and friendliness, of adventure or individualism wherever it raises its head. But we are preparing our children to be responsible citizens in a democracy, perhaps some day in a democratic world. Why then the screwed-down benches, the interdiction on speech, the marching through the halls in silent single-file, the injunction on the teacher to behave like a classroom Hitler?[102]

Take away the screwed-down benches and the silent marching and little has changed from the time of her writing to today. Control, however pleasantly administered, is control nevertheless and requires discounting of an individual's personal interests and needs along with the concomitant humiliation and shame delivered through rewards, grades, exhortations, and psychological or pharmacological manipulation.

More recently, John Gatto has written:

> Children learn what they live. Put kids in a class and they will live out their lives in an invisible cage, isolated from their chance at community; interrupt kids with bells and horns all the time and they will learn that nothing is important; force them to plead for the natural right to the toilet and they will become liars and toadies; ridicule them and they will retreat from human association; shame them and they will find a hundred ways to get even. The habits taught in large-scale organizations are deadly.[103]

And I add, finally, the deadly habits he mentions are not those of a democratic citizen.

---

[102] Caroline Pratt, *I Learn From Children*. (New York: Cornerstone Library Publications, 1948), 163.
[103] Gatto, *Dumbing Us Down*, 76.

Yeah, but what about ...

I can imagine the controversy already: What about those children who come from broken homes or from parents who are on drugs? Children whose young lives are already filled with anxiety and despair. Surely they will be emotionally damaged and need structure and professional help. What about those with learning disabilities or dyslexia, how are they ever going to learn anything if they aren't taught? What about those with special needs? Etc. etc. etc. These are arguments that I've heard proclaiming that freedom simply will not work for some children. I beg to differ. It is the structure, control, and discipline that exacerbate these problems. Problem kids are created by rules, authorities, and specialists, the result of over control and surveillance. The only adults they have ever associated with are unloving and disciplinary police, delinquent parents, or school people in positions of authority, directing and correcting.

It is not surprising that there are damaged kids and people out there given the dictatorial disciplinary methods of child-rearing that still prevail in some parts of society. Take, for example, John B. Watson's behaviorist views of baby and child care, [104] stressing the importance of rigid control, feeding schedules, and restricted contact. This "scientific" theory proposed that training for a tough and disciplined life must begin in infancy and any straying from regulation would lead to a "spoiled" child. "Spare the rod and spoil the child," which many people believe comes from the bible--(it doesn't[105])—is quoted as an excuse for beating and shaming a

---

[104] John B.Watson, *Psychological Care of Infant and Child*. (New York: W.W. Norton Company, Inc.. 1928)/

[105] Proverbs 13:24 (Authorized King James Version). "He that spareth his rod hateth his son: but he that loveth him chasteneth him betimes."

child. John Locke (1632-1704), whose influence can still be found everywhere, preached the denial of natural impulses: "Children should be used to submit their desires, and go without their longings, even from their very cradles"[106] It is assumed that a hard childhood prepares one for the rigours of adulthood, and the grim struggle of life will be driven by relentless ambition to succeed or consumed by rage and an urge to rebel and destroy.

Only a radical change in our treatment of babies and children will erase the damaging effects of past beliefs. Love is *unconditional* positive regard.

Freedom Again

By now, the reader will know that I favour social democracy (or democratic socialism) because that is what the school that is good for kids proposes. It means that freedom comes from having basic needs provided. These include government supported health care, dental care, housing, food security, public transportation, and all levels of education. There can be no freedom while some citizens live in poverty and misery while others have yachts, mansions, and the best of everything. There can be no freedom when people have to struggle to get their basic needs met. The inequality that has resulted from decades of a market-controlled economy has destroyed the lives and hopes of millions of people worldwide. A genuine social democracy must begin with freedom and self-determination for children and youth, not from an authoritarian regime that purports to know "what's good for you."

---

[106] John Locke, *Some Thoughts Concerning Education,* (originally published in 1693).

The six-year-old who sees that his or her thoughts and opinions are heard and valued as much as anyone else's will become an individual in a co-operative community where decisions are made by equal vote for the benefit of all. We learn that we don't always get our own way but that we benefit from the help and support of others. This will be as true in adulthood as it is in childhood. The goal is a society of co-operative individualism.

And That's All

What I am proposing in this book is a true revolution, a radical change from our beliefs about childhood and human nature. It means integrating children into society and recognizing their value as individuals. It means treating children—and each other—with respect, acceptance, and love. Imagine a society in which each person can grow, learn, and develop to their best individual potential. A society in which each person is equal.

To operate schools of this type would be expensive. However, much of the money that is now directed toward university departments of education, textbook writing and printing, standardized tests, school buildings that stand empty for months of every year, school boards, specialized staff, various experts, and research projects could now be spent directly on more educational staff, better equipment, and more benefits for children. Perhaps even some of the vast sums of money now going to space and defence programs could be reallocated to the education and well-being of our young. Isn't that where our future lies?

Will it ever happen? Probably not, at least not for some time. Social change happens slowly, and will only happen as people free themselves from the control of school and of corporate interests and place value on individual determinism in a co-operative society, a society in which each individual works for the common good. This will be a democratic society full of intelligent discourse, artistic expression, freedom, learning, and love of children.

APPENDIX

From: "Reginald on Worries" by Saki (H. H. Munro:

And then there's the Education Question—not that I can see that there's anything to worry about in that direction. To my mind education is an absurdly overrated affair. At least, one never took it very seriously at school, where everything was done to bring it prominently under one's notice. Anything that is worth knowing one practically teaches oneself, and the rest obtrudes itself sooner or later. The reason one's elders know so comparatively little is that they have to unlearn so much that they acquired by way of education before we were born.

Ed Broadbent:

In Canada today children are taught in schools throughout the land that our country is democratic primarily because there is more than one political party and because citizens have the right to criticize and the right to change their rulers every few years. This view of democracy, Mr. Speaker, is a distinctly modern phenomenon and is in marked contrast with the democracy of both the early Greeks and 19th century Europeans. Prior to our century democracy was seen by its defenders and critics alike as a kind of society in which all adults played an active, participatory role not only in the formal institutions of government but also in all the institutions which crucially affected their daily lives. Similarly a democratic society had been seen previously as one in which all its members had an equal opportunity to develop their capacities and talents; it was not seen as one in which citizens had an equal opportunity to earn more money or advance up the class ladder.

--Speech to the House of Commons, September 20, 1968

The School Boy   by William Blake

I love to rise in a summer morn,
When the birds sing on every tree;
The distant huntsman winds his horn,
And the sky-lark sings with me.
O! what sweet company.

But to go to school in a summer morn
O: it drives all joy away;
Under a cruel eye outworn.
The little ones spend the day.
In sighing and dismay.

Ah! then at times I drooping sit.
And spend many an anxious hour.
Nor in my book can I take delight,
Nor sit in learnings bower.
Worn thro' with the dreary shower.

How can the bird that is born for joy,
Sit in a cage and sing.
How can a child, when fears annoy,
But droop his tender wing.
And forget his youthful spring.

O! father & mother. if buds are nip'd,
And blossoms blown away.
And if the tender plants are strip'd
Of their joy in the springing day,
By sorrow and cares dismay.

How shall the summer arise in joy
Or the summer fruits appear,
Or how shall we gather what griefs destroy
Or bless the mellowing year.
When the blasts of winter appear

WHAT'S GOING ON AROUND HERE?
By Tom Durrie

When my brother was about three years old, so the family story goes, he was taken to a county fair, where he was given the enlightening opportunity of observing the various farm animals at close range. After twenty minutes or so of looking at cows, sheep, goats, chickens, and rabbits, his only comment was "What do we smell around here?"

I was reminded of this story when I recently spent four months directing a high school musical. The musical was *A Funny Thing Happened on the Way to the Forum* [107] and the high school was a small Catholic school of three hundred or so students in Grades 8 through 12. This was my second experience at this school; they produce a musical every second year. It's a major event for the school; parents and teachers get involved and a good deal of money is spent on theatre rent, costumes, sets, royalties, and a professional director. Like everything this school does—sports, debating teams, writing contests—the musical is a matter of pride in accomplishment. It is seen to establish the school's high reputation in the community.

Excitement was high when auditions were announced, and we had about a hundred kids hoping to get into the cast. Interestingly enough, and in my opinion to the school's credit, at least one third of the auditionees were

---

[107] *A Funny Thing Happened on the Way to the Forum*, music and lyrics by Stephen Sondheim, book by Burt Shevelove and Larry Gelbart, Music Theatre International, New York, 1962.

boys. Most but not all of the students were well prepared to audition. They were required to sing a song and to recite or read a selection of prose or poetry; the choice of what they were to perform was their own. Again to the school's credit, many of their choices showed a fair level of sophistication. We heard songs from Broadway musicals and movies, readings from Shakespeare, Donne, and the Bible. In this respect, it's worth noting that this is obviously a fairly select, I won't say elite, group of kids. Their parents are well-heeled enough to be able to afford a private school, many of these kids are outstandingly bright, and the school claims to maintain very high standards of discipline and of academic and other kinds of achievement.

When auditions were finished and casting completed, everyone involved in the musical was called to a special introductory meeting at which they were to have impressed upon them the seriousness of the commitment they were making. And serious it was since all rehearsals are held outside of regular school time and would be expected to take precedence over sports, music lessons, work, and other extracurricular activities. Rehearsals would be for an hour and a half, four days a week, right after school, with four full days during spring break, and long hours during the days before the show opened. We impressed upon them the importance of always being on time, being prepared with lines and songs learned when necessary, and of paying attention to the work at hand. During their one week spring break they would have to be available all day every day for intensive rehearsals. We also indicated that, where possible, we would adjust rehearsal calls to individual needs. For example, some of the boys were involved in a soccer tournament, others in a public speaking contest, and many of the boys and girls had part time jobs. Most of them as well were taking music or dance lessons, were involved in vari-

138

ous clubs or teams, and had regular homework assignments from their classes. The seriousness of the situation was made abundantly clear with threats that any sign of weakness in their academic work would result in their immediate expulsion from the cast. The principal or the school was in attendance at this meeting to lend an air of gravity to the proceedings.

After this, I worked out a detailed rehearsal schedule, indicating which scenes were to be worked on and who was required to be there week by week. Also, as I had done previously, I told the teachers with whom I would be working, as well as the principal, that although I knew a good deal about theatre and how to put on a good show, I did not "do discipline," and that I expected the exigencies of an impending performance would create an air of dedication and hard work. A delightful and energetic young woman, a teacher in the school, was assigned as full-time stage manager to work with me. It looked like rehearsals would be conducted in an atmosphere of decorous attentiveness.

As I mentioned earlier, I don't "do discipline." By this I mean that, though my Parent[108] is very good at deal-

---

[108] TA (Transactional Analysis) terms:
PARENT
     Nurturing Parent. Provides protection, loving care, and permission.
     Controlling Parent. That part of the psyche that controls or attempts to control by rules, advice, modeling, etc. Control, in this case, can be benevolent and helpful or dictatorial and destructive.
ADULT
     The Adult is freely thoughtful, reasoning, and learning from experience and authority, though always questioning. The Adult can also be contaminated by beliefs and rules, usually from the Controlling Parent.
CHILD
     Free Child. That part of us that is playful, curious, creative, and lovable.

ing with emergencies, insisting on good manners, and protecting the weak, I've never been able to find that element of Controlling Parent that can cause a classroom full of kids to stop talking, sit up straight, and pay attention. This might be a good thing because I tend to accept young people at face value, that is for what they are rather than what they might be if only I could whip them into shape. My Nurturing Parent delights in being with young people and observing their energy and growth, in spite of the fact that working with them sometimes drives me nuts. That is, it drives the part of my Parent that says "You really ought to be controlling these kids" nuts, while at the same time my Child, rebellious or otherwise, wants to horse around, be creative, and play. But also in my Parent (Parent in the Adult?) is a good and serious set of rules about the protocol of the theatre. I've had a lot of experience as an actor and a director. I've directed professional and amateur casts in plays, musicals, and operas, and as I said, I know how to put on a good show, and I know that it takes a lot of hard work to do it.

So, how was I going to accomplish the goal of a "good show" amid the chaos and insanity that rehearsals turned out to be? The serious talks about punctuality and good behaviour seem to have gone into one collective ear and out the other. Even the presence of the teacher/stage manager had little impact. Rarely was there a rehearsal attended by everyone who was supposed to be there, and often cast members arrived late, wandered in and out, consumed large quantities of candy and pop, and talked and laughed amongst themselves whenever they didn't have lines to say. This created a background of noise and confu-

---

Adapted Child. As the name suggests, adjusts behaviour, beliefs, and feelings to external (Controlling Parent) expectations and demands.

sion that made orderly work difficult to say the least. My teacher/stage manager often shook her head in dismay, but even her attempts at control were fruitless. Of course, a call for attention, usually made in a loud voice over the hubbub, would bring about thirty seconds or so of silence, quickly giving way to the usual racket. It soon became apparent that the kids could see no point in remaining quiet and attentive when they weren't actually part of the main action of a scene. The 16-year old boy who played the leading role had a way of simply wandering off after speaking a line, even if he were still supposed to be in the scene. A group of young girls, part of the chorus, who were directed to assume positions in the background and follow the action, would instead form a chatty little group, laughing and gossiping, about boys no doubt, combing each other's hair, etc. The part of the Captain was played by an athletic and handsome Grade 12 boy. He was 18. When he came to rehearsals—and that wasn't very often—he would stand around in a bored and tired manner, as though these proceedings were far beneath his capabilities and status. He didn't learn his lines until the day or so before the performances. The three other soldiers, small but important comic parts, were also played by Grade 12 boys. I had selected them especially for their comic potential. One was very tall, the school's star basketball player, the middle one was a strapping, mesomorphic lad, and the third was short, jolly, and rotund. The sight gag possibilities were limitless. During rehearsals they clowned around constantly, never staying where they were supposed to be, either talking to the girls, or manhandling each other in a way that reminded me of a group of bear cubs at play.

Once, the middle soldier said to me, "You know, we'd be much better if you'd yell at us," to which I replied,

"I don't yell at people." I think he meant that if I would yell and carry on in an angry, threatening manner, they would respond by being quiet and respectful. Speaking of which, there was never an instance of cheeky or ill-mannered behaviour on the part of any one of these young-sters. They always called me Mr. Durrie, and responded politely when spoken to individually. They may have been goofy and intractable, but they were never rude.

Occasionally, one or two would even apologize for causing disruption or for being late—and any serious late-ness or absence was always followed by a very reasonable explanation. They had to work, or baby-sit, or they were kept after school by another teacher, or they were playing in a tournament, or they were part of the school's public-speaking team, etc., etc. As I mentioned earlier, these kids are kept very busy, and each activity in which they are in-volved seems to have first claim on their time and attention. The fact that rehearsals often necessarily involve a lot of standing around and waiting, not to mention constant repe-tition, probably rated them on a lower scale of urgency in the minds of the youngsters. And this in spite of all the things that had been said to them at the start about how they were to give top priority to their participation in this musi-cal, etc., blah, blah, blah.

At one point, about three quarters of the way through the rehearsal period, we had a rebellion on our hands. At the end of rehearsal the day before, one of the boys asked me, very politely and reasonably, if they could start a half-hour or so late the next day because a well-known basketball player was coming to the school to talk and answer questions. As his request seemed perfectly jus-tified and sensible, I agreed. Later, however, when I con-veyed this information to the music teacher, he said he thought it would not be a good idea because it would give the kids the notion that they could have whatever they wanted. I thought hmmm, but said that after all the school was in charge here, and I would go along with whatever he and the principal decided. Well, they decided that the rehearsal should take place as scheduled.

At the appointed time on the day in question, only a handful of students turned up; these included the boy who had originally asked for the later starting time. He was very angry and upset, not only that he had been denied the opportunity to hear the basketball player, but also that he had come to rehearsal dutifully on time while many others had gone to the talk and, as we found out later, had simply gone on home afterwards. The rehearsal was, of course, a bust, since there weren't enough cast members there to do anything, and the fact that so many of the students had deliberately disobeyed orders meant the school was compelled to take some kind of action.

The action was to call each of the miscreants individually to the principal's office, where, I assume, they were given a stern talk. In some cases, I believe even the parents were informed of their offspring's misdeeds. All along, there had been talk of replacing anyone in the cast who proved to be uncooperative or erratic in attendance. There had also been threats made right from the start, that if any cast member showed a slacking off in academic work, they would immediately be dismissed from the cast and replaced. I'll have to say that we came very close to doing this several times, although I was most reluctant to give up any part of what I really felt was a perfect cast for this show. However, each time dismissal was considered to be imminent, the youngster in question came through with sincere apologies, statements about how much he or she wanted to be in the show, and so on. Consequently, all threats to the contrary notwithstanding, no one was ever dismissed or replaced.

Throughout all of this—and I hasten to add that the rehearsals went on for an inordinately long time, four months of an hour-and-a-half four afternoons a week!—I kept steadfastly to my program of blocking and rehearsing scenes, cooking up amusing business, polishing timing and diction, consulting over costumes and scenery, and meeting regularly with the music teacher, who was preparing the band and teaching the songs. I also found that however exasperating their behaviour might be, each of these kids was irresistibly appealing and engaging in his or her own way. It was always possible to talk with any of them individually; I enjoyed telling them stories and filling them in about various literary and other references in the script. I grew quite accustomed to their antic and erratic group actions and found them individually funny and endearing. The strapping 18-year-old in the part of the Captain actually brought a mattress and blankets to some of the all day rehearsals! It wouldn't have been surprising to see him cuddling a teddy bear or sucking his thumb. The older girls, though they had brought books and homework to various rehearsals, quickly formed into a group and chattered away, apparently delighted with each other's company and with that of the boys, with whom they associated freely and without coyness.

In our rehearsal room there was an electric organ, the kind that has built-in "chooch-a-doo" rhythms. Even though it was kept under a cover, and we asked them repeatedly not to touch it, several of the younger boys seemed incapable of leaving it alone, and we often found we were putting up with its insidious noise-making, although I must admit that it only formed a background to the general carryings on. And so it went. But after all, since it seemed they were being pulled in so many directions by so many "serious" concerns, I could at least provide them with an opportunity to find out who they really were. I was also impressed to notice that many of the older boys and girls owned and drove cars, so they must have been capable of some self-directed, goal-oriented, adult behaviour.

So how did it all turn out? At the end of the first complete run through with the band, held in the school gymnasium about a week before the show's opening, the cast applauded and cheered when I said, "I think you've got a show!" And, indeed, they did have a show. The four performances, presented in a local civic theatre seating 700, were nothing less than spectacular. I can only say that I could not have asked for or hoped for such energetic, dedicated, and concentrated performances by each member of the cast. The comic business came off without a hitch, entrances and exits were timed beautifully, properties held and used with professional aplomb, and the songs sung with genuine zest, abandon, and sincerity of expression. In other words, these youngsters with whom I had had what seemed like such a slap dash, tumultuous relationship for the past four months gave a performance that had professional polish, stage wise delivery, and a true sense of comedy and comic timing. So all along they really had been set on accomplishing the goal of a good, in fact great, show. As with getting a driver's licence or playing basketball, they were "goal-oriented." They just got to the goal of creating a brilliant performance in a different, unexpected way. While we might have expected to travel from point to point by driving smoothly down the freeway with everyone obeying the rules, they preferred to hack their way through the jungle, smelling the flowers, tearing their clothes, and skinning their knees along the way.

It is my custom to assemble the entire company about a half-hour before curtain time on opening night to give my pre-curtain speech. As the cast assembled in the green room, the three Grade 12 girls quietly took over, getting everyone to stand in a circle, hold hands, and concentrate on what was said. One of these girls, a very bright, buxom 18-year old who had appeared studiedly indifferent during rehearsals, spoke, asking the cast to dedicate their performance to a principal of the school who had died the previous year. She also spoke about the importance of giving your all, doing your best, and generally acquitting yourself in a manner that would be a credit to the entire group. The youngsters, under her leadership, then bowed their heads and fervently recited the Lord's Prayer. Need I say that I was profoundly touched and deeply moved; this was a side of these young people that I was not accustomed to seeing. When I spoke, after wiping away a few tears, I told them that people come to the theatre to experience something greater than and beyond their everyday lives, something that will bring them joy and renewed belief in the OKness of life. This was the gift that they, the actors and musicians, were going to bring to the audience. Then I said, "Many of you, you know, have been a pain in the ass throughout rehearsals, but I have grown very fond of each of you and working with you has been a very rewarding though sometimes difficult experience. I thank you for all you have given me."

On the second night, I came to them again, complimented them on the superb job they were all doing and then performed for them Hamlet's advice to the players. I said, "Everything you need to know about acting is right here." I explained to them who the "groundlings" were—some of the older students already knew this (*gratia dei* to a school that still teaches Shakespeare!)—and how easy it was to cheapen your performance by playing down to the audience. This is always a great fear with some non-professional actors, who as soon as they start hearing laughter from the audience, will start overdoing, clowning, mugging, etc., thinking they will get more laughs that way, and unfortunately they often do. The audience laughs, not at the character and situation in the play, but at the antics of the actor. As Hamlet says, "And let those that play your clowns speak no more than is set down for them; for there be of them that will themselves laugh, to set on some quantity of barren spectators to laugh too, though in the meantime some necessary question of the play be then to be considered."[109]

If I seem to be labouring this point, it's because I want to relate an incident that occurred during one of the performances. A boy of 16 or so had a small character part, that of a befuddled, near-sighted old man. He had been all but impossible during rehearsals, turning up late if at all, drawing attention to himself by joking and jostling with the other actors, not learning his lines, putting on a different sort of voice and character for each rehearsal, and so on. He was one of the ones we came very close to replacing. As we came closer to the dress rehearsal, I began to see a more consistent character emerge, but I was still afraid he would lose it completely when put before an audience. Surprise, surprise! He turned out a consistent and delightful characterisation that didn't vary from performance to performance. He showed a true sense of comedy without the slightest bit of overacting. One of the evening performances was attended by a group of his friends. They hooted and applauded every time he came on stage, reacting noisily to

---

[109] William Shakespeare: **The Tragedy of Hamlet, Prince of Denmark**, Act III, Scene ii.

his every move. Even a seasoned professional would have had difficulty maintaining concentration, but not this kid. As I said, his performance never varied, and his characterisation was a delight to watch. The greatest compliment you can get in theatre is to be called a "trouper", and that's exactly what this boy—and his fellow cast members—turned out to be: troupers.

So what was "going on around here"? Would these kids have turned out a better performance if they had quietly and respectfully listened to my every word, punctually attended every rehearsal, never talked to each other, and never touched the electric organ? I doubt it. In fact, I believe the opposite would have been the case. Acting, after all, is not just a matter of following directions. True, stage mechanics and blocking are matters of technique and direction that come from the Adult and Parent (Parent in the Adult), but performing is a matter for a liberated Free Child who can play in an intense and disciplined game of pretend. A "play" in the theatre is not unlike a "play" in sports, both require concentration, discipline, and free creative energy. Most kids, and many grownups, are good at playing games, because they can lose their self-awareness, self-consciousness, and let their Free Child play while at the same time observing the rules of the game and of fair play. In the theatre, on the other hand, the problem in working with most inexperienced actors is giving them enough powerful permission and protection to allow their Free Child to play. I would suggest that the period of relatively undisciplined—at least from the standpoint of what we used to call "deportment"—rehearsal, gave permission and protection to the Free Child in my cast of young actors.

This would be in marked contrast to what happens to them in the daily proceedings of school. I am proposing, in TA terms, that the purpose of school is to block out the

Free Child in favour of a Parent-contaminated Adult in an Adapted Child. The early years of school offer a crossed transaction that appears to be the teacher's Child to the youngster's Child: "Now we are going to read" "Now we are going to have recess" "This is how we sharpen our pencils" "This is how we line up at the door." The covert transaction is, of course, teacher's Controlling Parent to youngster's Adapted Child: "Do as I say, or you won't be one of us." In the later years of school, this acknowledged part of the transaction becomes teacher's Adult to youngster's Adult: "Doing well in school will assure you of a good job, entry into university, or whatever, later on." "Doing well in school will prepare you for the grown up world." The covert transaction remains Controlling Parent to Adapted Child, only now the threat is more serious: "You will be a failure as a grown up if you don't do what I say."

While this might sound a little harsh, it's important to remember a few basic principles. School sets the curriculum: it tells you what you are to learn and at what speed you are to learn it; it tells you when to eat, when to play, and when to go to the bathroom; it tells you when you can and you can't talk to your friends; it tells you what to sit on and how long to sit on it; and above all, it tells you to whom you are supposed to pay attention, who is more important than you are, and who knows more about running your life than you do. Alice Miller, in her remarkable book about the origins of violence *For Your Own Good*,[110] has coined the term "poisonous pedagogy" to refer to child rearing and educational practices that attempt to steer a

---

[110] Alice Miller: **For Your Own Good, Hidden cruelty in child-rearing and the roots of violence**, Farrar-Straus-Girouz, New York, 1983

child away from his or her natural, or Free Child, needs, interests, and pursuits. Her position is summed up in the Afterword to this book: "Conditioning and manipulation of others are always weapons and instruments in the hands of those in power even if these weapons are disguised with the terms *education* and *therapeutic treatment*." Enough said.

In a classic experiment conducted in 1950[111], rhesus monkeys were given mechanical puzzles to play with. The puzzles presented a problem of releasing a couple of retaining devices in order to free a moving hasp. The monkeys quickly mastered the puzzles and continued manipulating and playing with them, assembling and disassembling the devices over and over again. They quickly lost interest, however, when a food reward was given in response to a successful manipulation. This phenomenon was also observed in another experiment reported by Professor Harlow[112], "When the nonfood-rewarded animals had solved the puzzle, they frequently continued their explorations and manipulations. Indeed, one reason for the nonfood-rewarded monkeys' failure to achieve the experimenter's concept of a solution lay in the fact that the monkeys became fixated in exploration and manipulation of limited puzzle or puzzle-device components. From this point of view, hunger-reduction incentives may be regarded as motivation-destroying, not motivation supporting."

Without labouring the point or delving into the ethics of animal experiments, I think these examples support my conjecture that the introduction of Parent-supplied rewards or Parent-driven motives, has the direct effect of limiting Free Child curiosity and creativity, and of supporting

[111] Harry Frederick Harlow: **From Learning to Love, The Selected Papers of H. F. Harlow**, Ed. By Clara Mears Harlow, Praeger, New York, 1986, pp 77-86.
[112] Ibid., pp 95-96.

an Adapted Child willing to conform to or eager to rebel against Controlling Parent expectations. In either case, adaptation or rebellion, it is the Parent that's calling the shots.

While it is generally believed in our society that school is a beneficial institution, necessary and valuable to the rearing of our young, a considerable amount has been written expressing a contrary view. Ivar Berg, in his largely ignored but comprehensive study of education and jobs, concludes that school is a "licensing institution" because his investigators were told consistently by the corporate personnel managers they interviewed, " .. that diplomas and degrees were a good thing, that they were used as screening devices by which undesirable employment applicants could be identified and that the credentials sought were indicators of a personal commitment to 'good middle class values,' industriousness and seriousness of purpose as well as salutary personal habit and styles."[113] Exactly the reasons for attending school given in the sham Child to Child, Adult to Adult transactions masking the real Parent to Child transactions upon which school is based.

Without a doubt, a well-adjusted child with a strong feeling of being OK will go along with the joke, co-operate with the teacher/grown ups and even manage to pick up some useful learning along the way. But, I would suggest, the cost is great.

If "education" means producing, at best, literate, thoughtful, and articulate people who will go out and change the world, or at worst, self-directed, motivated people who will take charge of their own lives, engage in productive work, and function as members of communities, then the compulsory public school system has failed miser-

---

[113] Ivar Berg: **Education and Jobs, The Great Training Robbery**, Praeger, New York, 1970, p 78

ably in its job. I was reminded of this recently by an article in *The Vancouver Sun* which posed the question, "The Bible is being read less and less by people in North America. Is the trend part of decreasing religiosity, or is it just too hard to read?"[114] The author was, of course, referring to the Elizabethan language of the King James Version. Many schools, I hear, have also abandoned the reading and study of Shakespeare as being "too difficult." It's worth remembering that in the days before compulsory universal schooling, many children were taught to read from the Bible. But reading the Bible and Shakespeare, both foundations of Western culture, will not necessarily be of use to the corporate entities that are seeking employees with "good middle class values". Better that our job-seeker be ready and eager to climb the corporate ladder to higher position and wages than to go around questioning the basic assumptions of our culture. At providing this kind of product, the schools seem to be doing a fair job, even though Professor Berg's studies clearly show that degrees and diplomas do not make for productive and loyal employees, popular wisdom to the contrary notwithstanding.

But to get back to *A Funny Thing Happened on the Way to the Forum* (what an apt title, given the present observations—as any youngster might say about school 'A funny thing happened on the way to adulthood'). The students in the play, each of whom had had at least nine years of schooling, were accustomed to adults whose main goal was to control them, that is to engage them in a crossed transaction aimed at hooking their Adapted Child into some kind of behaviour, compliant or rebellious, appropriate to the school setting. Naively, perhaps, I approached them

---

[114] The Vancouver Sun, July 30, 1999, "The crises facing the Good Book" by Teresa Watanabe (re-printed from the Los Angeles Times.

saying, "We're going to put on a musical, you've decided to be in it, I know a lot about this kind of thing, and I'll help you do the good job I assume you want to do." This was my attempt to hook their Adult into accepting my authority, not as a bully but as an expert, and to engage their Child in what promised to be a lot of fun. Perceiving my straight transaction as a sign of weakness, they regarded me as a pushover, and proceeded to act up and carry on as they chose, perhaps trying to push me into becoming the familiar controlling adult. Curiously enough, several of the teachers expressed amazement at my patience, and noted that I had some of the most "difficult" kids in the school to work with. I hadn't really thought of it in this way. I don't like working in an atmosphere of noise and chaos any more than any other adult I know of. But my experience is that if you're going to try to accomplish something with a group of kids, and if you're not willing to be a bully, this is what you're going to get. Maybe it is the most efficient way after all.

This approach, for better or worse, allowed a lot of rambunctious Free Child to come into play. At the same time, a relationship of mutual appreciation and affection developed, as I allowed each young actor a lot of leeway in creating his or her own interpretation of the role, and helping matters along, they often had very good ideas for business and stage action, but respected my final say on what was to happen on stage. The whole process, in the final analysis, created a sense of cohesiveness and unity of purpose among a group of individual youngsters of various ages who, interestingly enough, were not used to associating with those outside of their own grade level. Though my Controlling Parent feels a bit beaten down by the experience ("You really ought to make those kids behave."), my

Nurturing Parent takes delight in having associated with such a challenging group of sparkling and loveable young-sters, and my Child is pleased as punch at having had an important part in creating a show that was so brilliant and entertaining.

After the final curtain of the last performance, I was called upon stage to receive the acknowledgement of the cast, parents, and teachers, and to receive flowers, a gift certificate, and a giant card made and signed by all the kids. The final words go to them:

> "Dear Mr. Durrie, I think you have the most enormous amount of patience of anyone I know! Thank you so much for making this play a suc-cess!"

> "Well, bud, it was fun. I still can't believe you put up with all our stuff. Thanks."

> "Woo-Hoo Mr. Durrie! Not only are you one of the guys on our "hot" list, but you can act too!"

> "You are awesome, thanks for putting up with me! You're the best. Love al-ways."

> Mr. Durrie, It was my first time having you as a director,

you're so great! I hope I made you proud of me. I was the best I could be. Love always."

Thanks for everything. You put up with a lot of stuff that other people would not and made this play what it really is."

Vancouver, British Columbia
August, 1999

REFERENCES

Allen, Marjory & Mary Nicholson, *Memoirs of an Uneducated Lady: Lady Allen of Hurtwood,* (London: Thames and Hudson Ltd, 1975).

Ariès, Philippe, *Centuries of Childhood, A Social History of Family Life, trans Robert Baldick*, (New York: Vintage Books, 1962).

Bob and Ray, Mr. Science No. 2, cut and paste: rb.gy/p5yuxa

Boden, Margaret, *Piaget*, (London: Fontana Press, 1994).

Bramham, Daphne, "Illiteracy exacts a grim toll around the world," The Vancouver Sun, Oct. 25, 2000.

Bransford, John D. et al, *How People Learn: Brain, Mind, Experience, and School (Expanded ed.),* (Washington, DC: National Academy Press. 2000).

Broadbent, Ed, *Seeking Social Democracy, Seven Decades in the Fight for Equality* (Toronto: ECW Press, 2023).

Buck, Naomi, "A Constant Distraction," *Globe and Mail*, September 2, 2023.

Canadian Broadcasting Corporation, *The Education Debates*, (Toronto: CBC Ideas Transcripts, 1998).

Christakis, Dimitri, "Media and Children," TEDx Talks, Dec. 29, 2011, YouTube Video, 16:11, https://www.google.com/search?client=firefox-b-d&q=Dimitri+Christakis#fpstate=ive&vld=cid:699c0c49,vid:BoT7qH_uVNo.

Christakis, Dimitri, "Media and Children," YouTube video, 0:16:11, December 28, 2011, https://www.youtube.com/watch?v=BoT7qH_uVNo&ab_channel=TEDxTalks.

Dewey, John, *The School and Society; The Child and the Curriculum, Reprint, Centennial edition*, (Chicago: University of *Chicago Press: 1990).*

Fidler, Richard, "One Room Schools A Hundred Years Ago: Of Study Time, Recitations, and Rec*ess*," Grand Traverse Journal, July 9, 2018, https://gtjournal.tadl.org/2018/one-room-schools-a-hundred-years-ago-of-study-time-recitations-and-recess/.

Flesch, Rudolf, *Why Johnny Can't Read—And What You Can Do About It* (New York: Harper and Brothers, 1955).

Gatto, John Taylor, *Dumbing us down: The hidden curriculum of compulsory schooling*. (Philadelphia: New Society Publishers, 1992).

Glasser, William, *The quality school: Managing students without coercion*, (New York: Harper & Row, 1990).

Gray, Peter, *Free to Learn, Why Unleashing the Instinct to Play Will Make Our Children Happier, More Self-Reliant, and Better Students for Life*, (New York: Basic Books, 2013).

Harlow, Harry F. & Donald R. Meyer, "Learning motivated by a manipulation drive," Journal of Experimental Psychology, 40,American Psychological Association, 1950.

Herndon, James, *How to Survive in Your Native Land*. (New York: Simon and Schuster, 1971).

Herrnstein, Richard J. & Charles Murray, *The bell curve: Intelligence and class structure in American life*, (New York: The Free Press, 1994).

Holt, John, *Growing Without Schooling (GWS)* video and audio documents about learning outside of school, homeschooling, self-directed learning, and the work of John Holt (1923-1985), https://www.youtube.com/@Johnholtgws/featured.

Holt, John, *How Children Learn, rev. ed.*. (New York, Delacorte Press: 1967).

Holt, John, *What do I do Monday?* (New York: E. P. Dutton & Co., Inc., 1970).

Hurtwood, Lady Allen, *Play and Playground Encyclopedia*, https://www.pgpedia.com/l/lady-allen-hurtwood.

Kohn, Alfie, *Punished by rewards: The trouble with gold stars, incentive plans, A's, praise, and other bribes*, Alfie, (New York: Houghton Mifflin Company, 1993)

Lashinsky, Wood, et al, *Scaling Organizations Panel, Software Conference*, accessed September 28, 2023, http://web.archive.org/web/20130729205322id_/http://itc.conversationsnetwork.org/shows/detail1033.html.

Locke, John, *Some Thoughts Concerning Education,* (originally published in 1693).

Menard, Louis, "The Elvic Oracle, Did anyone invent rock and roll?" (The New Yorker, November 8, 2015), https://www.newyorker.com/magazine/2015/11/16/the-elvic-oracle.

Ms Rachel - Toddler Learning Videos; Learn About Emotions and Feelings with Ms Rachel | Kids Videos | Preschool Learning Videos | Toddler
Copy and paste: rb.gy/rhrzbs

Nachmanovitch, Stephen, *Free Play: Improvisation in life and art*, (New York: Tarcher/Putnam, 1990).

Negroponte, Nicholas, *Being Digital.* (New York: Alfred A. Knopf, Inc, 1995)

Neill, Alexander Sutherland, *"Neill, Neill, Orange Peel!" An autobiography by A.S. Neill*, (New York: Hart Publishing Company, Inc, 1972).

Neill, Alexander Sutherland, *Summerhill, A Radical Approach to Childrearing*, (New York: Hart Publishing Company: 1960).

Neill, Alexander Sutherland, *The Free Child*, (London: Herbert Jenkins: 1953).

Neill, Alexander Sutherland, *Summerhill: A radical approach to child rearing*. New York: Hart Publishing Company Inc., 1960).

Office for Standards in Education (Ofsted), "School Report, Summerhill School,"
https://files.ofsted.gov.uk/v1/file/50075777/.

Pink, Daniel H., *Drive, the surprising truth about what motivates us*, (New York: Riverhead Books, 2009), 185.

Postman, Neil, *The disappearance of childhood*, (New York: Vintage Books, 1982).

Pratt, Caroline, *I Learn from Children*. (New York: Cornerstone Library Publications, 1948), 14-15

Pratt, Caroline, *I Learn From Children*. (New York: Cornerstone Library Publications, 1948),

Proverbs 13:24 (Authorized King James Version), "He that spareth his rod hateth his son: but he that loveth him chasteneth him betimes."

Putnam, Robert D., *Bowling Alone*, (Journal of Democracy, John Hopkins University Press, 6:1),

Putnam, Robert D., *Bowling Alone, The Collapse and Revival of American Community*, (New York: Simon & Schuster Paperbacks, 2000).

Rousseau, Jean Jacques, *Emile or On Education, trans Allan Bloom*, (New York: Basic Books Inc, 1979), Original published in 1762.

Shaw, George Bernard, *The London Times*, August 2, 1944. cited in Allen (1975).

Smith, Frank, *The Book of Learning and Forgetting*. (New York: Teachers College Press. 1998).

Smith, Frank, *Understanding Reading, A Psycholinguistic Analysis of Reading and leaning to Read* (New York: Holt, Rinehart and Winston, 1971).

Spock, Dr. Benjamin, *Baby and Child Care*, (New York: Pocket Books, Inc. 1946).

Stackhouse, John, "Planet America: The Eureka Formula.") (Toronto: *The Globe and Mail* , Oct. 18, 2000),

Stanley Greenspan, *The Growth of the Mind: And the Endangered Origins of Intelligence*, (Reading, MA: Addison Wesley: 1997).

Sternberg, Robert J., *Successful Intelligence: How Practical and Creative Intelligence Determine Success in Life*, (New York: Simon & Schuster, 1996).

Summerhill School, A. S. Neill Summerhill School, https://www.summerhillschool.co.uk/freedom-not-licence.

Thompson, Derek, "Presidential Speeches Were Once College-Level Rhetoric—Now They're for Sixth-Graders," (The Atlantic, Oct. 14, 2014). https://www.theatlantic.com/politics/archive/2014/10/have-presidential-speeches-gotten-less-sophisticated-over-time/381410/.

UNESCO, *Technology in Education: A Tool on Whose Terms*, Global Education Monitoring Report 2023.

Vygotsky, Lev, *Mind in Society, The Development of Higher Psychological Processes*, ed. Michael Cole, Vera John-Steiner, Sylvia Scribner, Ellen Souberman, (Cambridge, MA: Harvard University Press, 1978).

Watson, John B., *Psychological Care of Infant and Child.* (New York: W.W. Norton Company, Inc.. 1928)/

Zander, Benjamin, "The transformative power of classical music," TED2008, YouTube video, 20:22, https://www.ted.com/talks/benjamin_zander_the_transformative_power_of_classical_music?language=en.

WEBSITES REFERENCED
BC's Course Curriculum," (2015), https://curriculum.gov.bc.ca/.

"Mobile phone usage among children and teens in Canada as of April 2022, by age group," accessed September 19, 2023, https://www.statista.com/statistics/1319950/canada-mobile-usage-kids-and-teens-by-age/

https://www.google.com/search?client=firefox-b-d&q=Class+Dojo

"Adventure Playgrounds, a children's world in the city," http://adventureplaygrounds.hampshire.edu/history.html , accessed June 17, 2023.

https://www.youtube.com/user/scishowkids